Printed in Canada by Hemlock Printers

Contact: contact@first15.org
www.first15.org

Designed by Matt Ravenelle
mattravenelle.com

ABOUT FIRST15

Spending time alone with God every day can be a struggle. We're busier – and more stressed – than ever. But still, we know it's important to spend time alone with our Creator. We know we need to read his word, pray, and worship him.

First15 bridges the gap between desire and reality, helping you establish the rhythm of meaningful, daily experiences in God's presence. First15 answers the critical questions:

• Why should I spend time alone with God?
• How do I spend time alone with God?
• How do I get the most out of my time alone with God?
• How can I become more consistent with my time alone with God?

And by answering these questions through the format of daily devotionals, you'll practice the rhythm of meeting with God while experiencing the incredible gift of his loving presence given to those who make time to meet with him.

Allow God's passionate pursuit to draw you in across the next several days. And watch as every day is better than the last as your life is built on the solid foundation of God's love through the power of consistent, meaningful time alone with him.

To learn more about First15, visit our website first15. org. First15 is available across mobile app, email, podcast, and our website. Subscribe to our devotional today and experience God in a fresh way every day.

———————

CONTENTS

The Holy Spirit

"The Helper, the Holy Spirit, whom the Father will send in my name, he will teach you all things, and bring to your remembrance all that I said to you." John 14:26

WEEKLY OVERVIEW

As believers, we've been given the Holy Spirit as a Helper, Teacher, Friend, and seal for the promised inheritance of eternal life with God. His presence, guidance, and wisdom in our lives are our greatest gifts while here on earth. Through him we have access to direct connection with our heavenly Father. Through him we receive spiritual gifts to empower us. And through him we are able to bear the incredible fruit of abundant life. Open your heart and mind to all that the Holy Spirit would give you, show you, and lead you to this week.

The Leading of the Holy Spirit

DAY 1

DEVOTIONAL

Where do you need leadership in your life? What challenge, decision, or circumstance is weighing on you? Where do you need a word from God today? We have available to us the most perfect guide to lead us throughout the twists, turns, and challenges of this adventurous life. The Bible says in Romans 8:14, *"For all who are led by the Spirit of God are sons of God."* As children of the Most High God, we are granted full access to the leadership of the Holy Spirit who dwells within us. No child of God is exempt from the leadership of the Spirit. We don't earn access by our own merit. We don't gain more favor to receive more leadership. God has given us all the gift of the Holy Spirit because he loves us. He has filled us with his Spirit because he longs to lead us into the abundant life he has planned for us. So, let's learn today how we can better discover and follow this gift of leadership we've all been granted through Christ in the Holy Spirit.

*"For all who are led by the
Spirit of God are sons of God."*

ROMANS 8:14

First, it's crucial to acknowledge that the Holy Spirit and the word work perfectly together. One does not contradict the other. Both the Holy Spirit and the word he inspired are vital in living the Christian life. And God's word says in Galatians 5:16-18, *"But I say, walk by the Spirit, and you will not gratify the desires of the flesh. For the desires of the flesh are against the Spirit, and the desires of the Spirit are against the flesh, for these are opposed to each other, to keep you from doing the things you want to do. But if you are led by the Spirit, you are not under the law."* The leadership of the Spirit is in direct opposition to the lifestyle of the world. His desire is always to lead us away from sin that entangles us in the perspectives and pressures of the world toward a lifestyle of peace, joy, and intimate relationship with our heavenly Father. All of his leadership is purposed toward the goal of abundant life in God, of the fullness of satisfaction in God rather than the weak and fleeting pleasure in things of the world.

So how do we follow this person of the Holy Spirit toward that abundant life? Galatians 5:25 says, *"If we live by the Spirit, let us also keep in step with the Spirit."* How do we *"keep in step with the Spirit"*? It all starts with spending time getting to know what the Holy Spirit is like. He has a personality. He has a voice. His leadership feels a certain way. Just as you get to know a person, you can get to know the Holy Spirit. And the absolute best way to learn about him is one-on-one. Often we wait until we are in public, or right before a highly stressful situation, to ask for the guidance of the Spirit. But it's in the secret place that we learn what his voice and leading sounds and feels like so that we can discern his guidance out in the rush and stress of the world. It's in the secret place that we grow in relationship with the Holy Spirit so that we can follow his steps throughout the twists and turns of our day.

John 16:13 says, *"When the Spirit of truth comes, he will guide you into all the truth, for he will not speak on his own authority, but whatever he hears he will speak, and he will declare to you the things that are to come."* The Holy Spirit is excited to speak to you what he hears from the heavenly Father. He longs to declare to you God's plans to love you, provide for you, heal you, transform you, and deliver you. He longs to lead you to the fullness of life available to you here. Spend time getting to know the Holy Spirit in the secret place today. As you pray ask God to reveal himself to you. Spend time in prayer resting in the presence of the God who dwells within you, who is nearer to you than the very ground beneath your feet.

14

GUIDED PRAYER

1. Meditate on God's desire to lead you into abundant life.

"For all who are led by the Spirit of God are sons of God." Romans 8:14

"The thief comes only to steal and kill and destroy. I came that they may have life and have it abundantly." John 10:10

2. Ask the Holy Spirit to reveal himself to you. Spend time learning about who he is. Ask him to speak to you and to reveal the way his leadership feels.

"The Spirit himself bears witness with our spirit that we are children of God." Romans 8:16

"When the Spirit of truth comes, he will guide you into all the truth, for he will not speak on his own authority, but whatever he hears he will speak, and he will declare to you the things that are to come." John 16:13

"While they were worshiping the Lord and fasting, the Holy Spirit said, 'Set apart for me Barnabas and Saul for the work to which I have called them.'" Acts 13:2

"For it has seemed good to the Holy Spirit and to us to lay on you no greater burden than these requirements." Acts 15:28

3. Open up your life to the Holy Spirit. Ask him to reveal to you things he wants to lead you away from. Ask him to show you the life he wants to lead you to. And commit to following his leadership today.

"But I say, walk by the Spirit, and you will not gratify the desires of the flesh. For the desires of the flesh are against the Spirit, and the desires of the Spirit are against the flesh, for these are opposed to each other, to keep you from doing the things you want to do. But if you are led by the Spirit, you are not under the law." Galatians 5:16-18

When you have opportunities to indulge in the flesh, choose life in the Spirit instead. When you feel a desire to avenge yourself, promote yourself, slander someone, or engage in a sinful activity, choose life in the Spirit instead. Choose to love God and others. Live in step with the Spirit and discover the amazing life he longs to guide you into today.

Extended Reading: Romans 8

Friendship with the Holy Spirit

DAY 2

DEVOTIONAL

In friendship with the Holy Spirit we begin to experience a sense of wholeness and joy unattainable through any other relationship or aspect of life. Rapid and wonderful transformation results when you discover the wealth of love that comes with continual, real friendship with the living God. In friendship with God comes peace, security, honesty, healing, and freedom.

As you live your life in step with the Spirit, you experience what Adam and Eve experienced as they walked with God himself in the Garden of Eden. You discover the vast reservoir of love, affection, and perfect help that's available to you in the Holy Spirit. Open your heart today to receive a fresh revelation of God's desire for friendship with you through the Holy Spirit.

"The friendship of the Lord is for those who fear him, and he makes known to them his covenant."

PSALM 25:14

Jesus says in John 15:15, *"No longer do I call you servants, for the servant does not know what his master is doing; but I have called you friends, for all that I have heard from my Father I have made known to you."* God longs for friendship with his people. And through the Holy Spirit we have a continual connection with God available to us. The Spirit desires to do life with you. He wants to guide you, speak to you, and love you. He wants to satisfy your longing for relationship and can do so in greater ways than you can imagine.

John 14:16-17 says, *"And I will ask the Father, and he will give you another Helper, to be with you forever, even the Spirit of truth, whom the world cannot receive, because it neither sees him nor knows him. You know him, for he dwells with you and will be in you."* By God's grace you have been filled with God himself. You have dwelling with you the same Spirit who authored Scripture, raised Christ from the dead, empowered the disciples, and hovered over the waters at the creation of all things. And Scripture says that he longs to help you! Jesus calls him the *"Helper."* How incredible is the grace of our God to offer us relationship with the Holy Spirit! How great is his love that he would send his Son to die that we might have abundant life for all of eternity, including right now!

So, how do we grow in friendship with the Holy Spirit? How do we allow him to satisfy our desire for relationship? Psalm 25:14 says, *"The friendship of the Lord is for those who fear him, and he makes known to them his covenant."* And Ephesians 4:30 says, *"And do not grieve the Holy Spirit of God, by whom you were sealed for the day of redemption."* Friendship with the Holy Spirit starts like any other true friendship. We must respect, love, and make time for him. We must learn what he likes and dislikes. And we must apologize when we do something that hurts him. The Holy Spirit has feelings like any other person. But he is also full of grace, forgiveness, and unconditional love. Friendship with him comes about by following his leadership, making time to ask him how he feels about things, and following his guidance away from a lifestyle of sin into the righteousness available to you through Christ Jesus.

The Holy Spirit is waiting right now to guide you into friendship with him. He's excited about the idea of pouring out his love and affections on you. He longs to lead you away from the sins that hurt you and grieve him. And he longs to guide you toward a life of walking with him in relationship. Spend time in prayer being filled with the Holy Spirit afresh and making room to discover the reality of his presence in your life.

17

GUIDED PRAYER

1. Meditate on God's desire for friendship with you.

"No longer do I call you servants, for the servant does not know what his master is doing; but I have called you friends, for all that I have heard from my Father I have made known to you." John 15:15

"The friendship of the Lord is for those who fear him, and he makes known to them his covenant." Psalm 25:14

2. Ask the Holy Spirit to pour his love out on you. Ask him to make the reality of his nearness known to you. Be filled with desire to live your life in relationship with this real, tangible God who loves you.

3. Ask the Holy Spirit what he likes and doesn't like. Open your life and let him speak to you about whatever is causing you trouble.

Ask him how he feels about relationships, situations, thoughts, and perspectives you have. The Spirit loves to speak to us and help us.

"And I will ask the Father, and he will give you another Helper, to be with you forever, even the Spirit of truth, whom the world cannot receive, because it neither sees him nor knows him. You know him, for he dwells with you and will be in you." John 14:16-17

Often we separate out what we think God cares about and what just seems to be normal, worldly parts of life. But God wants to be involved in every part of our lives. He wants to be there for us in everything we do. He wants to fill us with grace and joy to do all the things set before us, from taking out the trash to washing dishes to leading thousands of people in prayer. Allow the Holy Spirit to come in and work in every area of your life and discover the wealth of knowledge and love your God has to share with you.

Extended Reading: John 14

Praying with the Holy Spirit

DAY 3

DEVOTIONAL

God loves to respond to the prayers of his people. We see him respond to the desire of Adam for a helpmate with Eve, the prayer of Abraham in saving Lot and his family, the prayer of Moses in the salvation of his people, the prayer of Elijah in sending down fire upon an altar, and the cry for a Savior in sending his only son, Jesus. And through the death of Jesus we've been filled with the Holy Spirit, God himself sent as our Helper. Our Helper not only longs to guide us and empower us, but also to help us pray and to pray for us.

Jude 1:20-21 says, *"But you, beloved, building yourselves up in your most holy faith and praying in the Holy Spirit, keep yourselves in the love of God, waiting for the mercy of our Lord Jesus Christ that leads to eternal life."* We've been given the incredible gift of praying with the Holy Spirit. The Spirit who searches the deep things of God desires to help us pray. He desires to reveal God's desires to us in the midst of our circumstances, relationships, and opportunities and longs to help us pray in line with

"But you, beloved, building yourselves up in your most holy faith and praying in the Holy Spirit, keep yourselves in the love of God, waiting for the mercy of our Lord Jesus Christ that leads to eternal life."

JUDE 1:20-21

God's will. When we pray in the Spirit we are praying along with the will of God himself. When we pray in the Spirit we are asking God to do the very thing he desires to do. It's crucially important that we as children of God learn how to discern the will of our Father through the Holy Spirit and pray according to that will.

Matthew 21:22 says, *"And whatever you ask in prayer, you will receive, if you have faith."* And Romans 10:17 teaches us, *"So faith comes from hearing, and hearing through the word of Christ."* Scripture tells us to pray in full faith that God will give us what we ask for because faith is always meant to begin with the word of God. Prayer is meant to be as simple as asking God to fill us with the knowledge of his desire and then praying in accordance with that desire in full faith because God will always fulfill his promises.

What's more, when we don't know what to pray we can trust in and lean on the groanings of the Spirit. Romans 8:26 says, *"Likewise the Spirit helps us in our weakness. For we do not know what to pray for as we ought, but the Spirit himself intercedes for us with groanings too deep for words."* Did you know that the Holy Spirit prays for you? Did you know that he intercedes on your behalf? So great is his love for you that he asks God to help you. So great is his desire for you to walk in abundant life that he intercedes on your behalf when you don't know how to pray.

Aren't you thankful for the grace of God? In his grace he's blessed you with the Holy Spirit to help you pray and intercedes for you, all because he loves you. You've been given an incredible, powerful gift in praying with the Holy Spirit. Take time today to listen to your Helper as you enter into a time of prayer.

GUIDED PRAYER

1. Meditate on the Spirit's desire to help you pray and to intercede for you.

"But you, beloved, building yourselves up in your most holy faith and praying in the Holy Spirit, keep yourselves in the love of God, waiting for the mercy of our Lord Jesus Christ that leads to eternal life." Jude 1:20-21

"Likewise the Spirit helps us in our weakness. For we do not know what to pray for as we ought, but the Spirit himself intercedes for us with groanings too deep for words. And he who searches hearts knows what is the mind of the Spirit, because the Spirit intercedes for the saints according to the will of God." Romans 8:26-27

2. Ask the Spirit to fill you with the knowledge of God's will for whatever it is you desire to pray about. Before you speak, listen.

3. Pray in line with what the Spirit has revealed to you. Ask God, in faith, to bless you with whatever you feel he has shown you. Pray along with Scripture! Rest in the assurance that

God will provide you with any and every thing that is in his perfect will for you when you ask him to.

"And whatever you ask in prayer, you will receive, if you have faith." Matthew 21:22

"So faith comes from hearing, and hearing through the word of Christ." Romans 10:17

God loves to make the Christian life simpler than we often make it out to be. I used to believe that to discover God's will I had to ask God for things and wait to see if life's circumstances panned out in line with those prayers. But God longs to fill us with the knowledge of his will even before you ask so that we can simply pray in full faith and joy in accordance with what he already desires to do. He blesses us with a life of simplicity if we will simply, wholeheartedly follow him. Take time today to search out the will of God for your life and rest in assurance of his faithfulness as you pray.

Extended Reading: Hebrews 11

Being Taught by the Holy Spirit

DAY 4

DEVOTIONAL

We have in the Holy Spirit the same Teacher who faithfully breathed the perfect and practical words of Scripture to imperfect men across thousands of years. And Jesus said in John 14:26, *"But the Helper, the Holy Spirit, whom the Father will send in my name, he will teach you all things and bring to your remembrance all that I have said to you."* Not only did the Holy Spirit teach the disciples, but he also longs to teach us. He longs to reveal to us the depths of God so that we might learn what it is to be a true follower of our Lord, Jesus Christ. He longs to show us the wisdom of God so that we

might live as men and women inspired by God rather than fools who find their knowledge only in the matters of the world. Let's open our minds and hearts to receive the wisdom that can only come from God himself in the Holy Spirit.

Paul writes in 1 Corinthians 2:10, *"These things God has revealed to us through the Spirit. For the Spirit searches everything, even the depths of God."* The Holy Spirit who dwells within us searches the depths of God and longs to reveal to us the ways of our heavenly Father. He longs to teach

*"But you have been anointed
by the Holy One, and you all
have knowledge."*

1 JOHN 2:20

us what it is to be a lover of God in a world set in opposition to the ways of God. He longs to reveal to us the wisdom of God's plans and show us the folly that comes from living for the world.

The Holy Spirit desires to be your Teacher today. The questions before you today are: are you willing to be his student? Are you willing to submit your understanding to the Holy Spirit and live in light of his teaching? Are you willing to appear foolish at times when the world doesn't understand the wisdom of God? Are you willing to live wholeheartedly for the pleasure of your heavenly Father over the fleeting opinions of man? If you will open your heart and mind today to being taught by the Spirit, you will discover a wealth of truth that has the power to set you free from the bonds and burdens of this world. Scripture will begin to change your life as the Holy Spirit reveals to you how these words written thousands of years ago are entirely applicable to your life today.

Receiving the teaching of the Holy Spirit is as simple as submitting our lives to him one day at a time and making time to listen to him and study the word with him. As important and helpful as they are, we

don't have to be pastors, ministers, theologians, or scholars to understand what the Bible means. The Holy Spirit will be our teacher the way he was for the disciples. He will teach us how Scripture applies to our life and guide us into the way of truth. It's incredibly important that we make time to study Scripture, but it's equally important that we read the Bible along with the Spirit instead of apart from him. The Bible is a practical book meant to impact the lives of those who read it under the influence of the Spirit. It's a manual for living life in the abundance of relationship with God, not a book to be read apart from the reality of God's nearness. Scripture is meant to guide us into direct communication with our heavenly Father, not substitute real, direct relationship with him.

Proverbs 3:5–6 says, *"Trust in the Lord with all your heart, and do not lean on your own understanding. In all your ways acknowledge him, and he will make straight your paths."* Trust in the teaching of the Holy Spirit today. Lean on his wisdom instead of your own. Acknowledge the reality of his nearness in your life. And discover knowledge that has the power to fill you with abundant life.

GUIDED PRAYER

1. Meditate on the Holy Spirit's desire to be your teacher.

"But the Helper, the Holy Spirit, whom the Father will send in my name, he will teach you all things and bring to your remembrance all that I have said to you." John 14:26

"But you have been anointed by the Holy One, and you all have knowledge." 1 John 2:20

2. Choose to be a student of the Holy Spirit. Choose to follow what he reveals to you to be wisdom over the ways of the world. Choose his opinion over man's.

"Trust in the Lord with all your heart, and do not lean on your own understanding. In all your ways acknowledge him, and he will make straight your paths." Proverbs 3:5-6

"But the anointing that you received from him abides in you, and you have no need that anyone should teach you. But as his anointing teaches you about everything, and is true, and is no lie—just as it has taught you, abide in him." 1 John 2:27

3. Spend time studying Scripture with the Holy Spirit. Pray and ask the Spirit to reveal to you what wisdom he wants to show you. Ask him to show you the meaning of the words you are reading. Allow him to apply Scripture directly to your life.

"These things God has revealed to us through the Spirit. For the Spirit searches everything, even the depths of God." 1 Corinthians 2:10

"If any of you lacks wisdom, let him ask God, who gives generously to all without reproach, and it will be given him." James 1:5

We have perfectly powerful guidance in Scripture and the Holy Spirit. The pairing of God's written word and the very God who authored the word have the power to lead us into a life of all wisdom, understanding, and revelation. But we must choose to live this life in light of eternity. We must choose success in heaven over success in the world's eyes. Scripture and the teaching of the Holy Spirit only have power in our lives if we follow their leadership and principles. Choose today to be a doer of the word instead of a hearer only and discover freeing and empowering wisdom that has the power to transform your life.

Extended Reading: 1 John 2

The Fruit of the Holy Spirit

DAY 5

DEVOTIONAL

The fruit of the Spirit passage in Galatians 5:22-23 gives me tremendous hope for my own life. Scripture says, *"But the fruit of the Spirit is love, joy, peace, patience, kindness, goodness, faithfulness, gentleness, self-control; against such things there is no law."* When I read that list I receive a vision of who I long to be. I long to be a person full of love, joy, and peace. I long to have patience, kindness, and goodness. I long to be marked by faithfulness, gentleness, and self-control. Who wouldn't? I see within those incredible characteristics the marks of a fully abundant life. I see Jesus.

"But the fruit of the Spirit is love, joy,
peace, patience, kindness, goodness,
faithfulness, gentleness, self-control;
against such things there is no law."

GALATIANS 5:22-23

At the same time, I see myself in light of these incredible fruits of the Spirit. I see all the ways in which my life doesn't line up with what the Holy Spirit desires to birth in me. How can we, in all our sin and brokenness, live a life marked by these characteristics? How can we be a people so full of the Spirit that our very being portrays the Spirit of God who dwells within us?

God longs to tell you and me today that by his grace, a life marked by the fruit of the Spirit is entirely possible—but only by his grace. In and of myself, I can produce none of these wonderful characteristics. In my own strength, I will only produce selfishness, laziness, and pride. *"But with God all things are possible"* (Matthew 19:26). The Bible calls these characteristics fruit for a reason. They are birthed out of the glorious working of God in us. They come entirely by God's grace.

So how do we allow the Holy Spirit to work at the core of our being and produce these wonderful fruits? How do we become children of God marked by the working of the Spirit in our lives? It comes from being connected to our source, that he might plant seeds that grow within us. As we spend time with God we become like him. In his presence our heart transforms into a greater reflection of his glorious love. He can do incredible and miraculous things in us if we simply open our hearts and spend time abiding in him. The more time we spend receiving his love for us, the more areas of brokenness and sin become healed and transformed. If you want to bear the fruit of the Spirit—if you want to be a person marked by the working of God at your core—then you must spend time each day simply being loved by God.

There is no shortcut to holiness. There is no trick to godliness. Jesus has made a way for us to enter into the holy places and see the face of God. God will do magnificent things in you today if you will follow the path laid before you by Jesus and spend time resting in the presence of your heavenly Father. Receive his love. Allow the words he speaks over you to transform the way you view yourself and the world around you. Spend time in prayer meditating on his word and allowing your heart to become more like Jesus' today.

29

GUIDED PRAYER

1. Meditate on God's desire and ability to produce the fruit of the Spirit in you. Allow his word to fill you with hope that you can be a person marked by these characteristics.

"But the fruit of the Spirit is love, joy, peace, patience, kindness, goodness, faithfulness, gentleness, self-control; against such things there is no law." Galatians 5:22-23

"Blessed is the man who walks not in the counsel of the wicked, nor stands in the way of sinners, nor sits in the seat of scoffers; but his delight is in the law of the Lord, and on his law he meditates day and night. He is like a tree planted by streams of water that yields its fruit in its season, and its leaf does not wither. In all that he does, he prospers. The wicked are not so, but are like chaff that the wind drives away. Therefore the wicked will not stand in the judgment, nor sinners in the congregation of the righteous." Psalm 1:1-5

2. Receive God's presence and rest in his love. Open up any broken places in your life to him. Talk to him about any areas in which you consistently struggle with sin and allow his love to heal those wounds.

3. Ask the Holy Spirit to bear fruit in you today. Ask him to lead you to a lifestyle of love, joy, and peace. Ask him to fill you with patience, kindness, and goodness toward others and yourself. Ask him to make you a person marked by faithfulness, gentleness, and self-control.

It's vital that you understand these characteristics are not something you strive toward in your own strength, but they are a natural result of being loved by God. You will never be able to be consistently faithful, gentle, or anything else good in your own strength. It takes the work of the Spirit to be marked by the Spirit. Engage with the Holy Spirit throughout your day. When you find yourself in a situation and are struggling to be a person full of the fruit of the Spirit, take a minute and ask for the Holy Spirit's help. Ask him to share with you his perspective and heart. He is with you in every moment and longs to help you live your life to the fullest. Enjoy his love today and live your life out of the abundance of God's presence available to you.

Extended Reading: Galatians 5

Sanctification in the Holy Spirit

DAY 6

DEVOTIONAL

The word "sanctification" typically renders images of fire, struggle, pain, and toil in my mind. It makes me think of my own sin and wonder how I could ever be transformed into a sanctified child of God. I believe sanctification is one of those words commonly used within the church but often misunderstood. We might understand the definition of sanctification (the process of being made or becoming holy), but I don't know if we have fully grasped God's plan for the process. I don't know if we've been taught on sanctification in light of God's grace.

1 Peter 1 gives us wonderful insight into God's heart for the process of sanctification:

Peter, an apostle of Jesus Christ,

To those who are elect exiles of the Dispersion in Pontus, Galatia, Cappadocia, Asia, and Bithynia, according to the foreknowledge of God the Father, in the sanctification of the Spirit, for obedience to Jesus Christ and for sprinkling with his blood:

May grace and peace be multiplied to you.

Blessed be the God and Father of our Lord Jesus Christ! According to his great mercy, he has caused us to be born again to a living hope through the resurrection of Jesus Christ from the dead, to an inheritance that is imperishable, undefiled, and unfading, kept in heaven for you, who by God's

*"According to the foreknowledge of God the Father,
in the sanctification of the Spirit, for obedience to
Jesus Christ and for sprinkling with his blood:
May grace and peace be multiplied to you."*

1 PETER 1:2

power are being guarded through faith for a salvation ready to be revealed in the last time. In this you rejoice, though now for a little while, if necessary, you have been grieved by various trials, so that the tested genuineness of your faith—more precious than gold that perishes though it is tested by fire—may be found to result in praise and glory and honor at the revelation of Jesus Christ. Though you have not seen him, you love him. Though you do not now see him, you believe in him and rejoice with joy that is inexpressible and filled with glory, obtaining the outcome of your faith, the salvation of your souls (1 Peter 1:1–9).

The first thing we see in 1 Peter 1:2 is that sanctification is *"of the Spirit."* Sanctification comes from God working in us, not from our own strength. In fact, Scripture is clear that righteousness is ours as the result of the life, death, and resurrection of Christ. 1 Corinthians 6:11 says, *"You were washed, you were sanctified, you were justified in the name of the Lord Jesus Christ and by the Spirit of our God."* And 2 Peter 1:3 says, *"His divine power has granted to us all things that pertain to life and godliness, through the knowledge of him who called us to his own glory and excellence."* Sanctification comes from God's work and power. In our own strength we can't produce anything like sanctification because we have

no holiness within ourselves. But in the Holy Spirit we have access to a vast, deep well of righteousness and godliness. Through Christ we've been made clean, and through the work of the Holy Spirit we are growing up into a life of holiness.

1 Peter 1 is most definitely clear that sanctification is a tough process. Dealing with our sin will never be easy. But it is a process full of the work of our merciful God (1 Peter 1:3), and it always results in rejoicing (1 Peter 1:8).

If you desire holiness, righteousness, and godliness, seek out relationship with the Holy Spirit. Open your heart and mind to his work. Allow him to reveal to you the dark places of your heart that have yet to be touched by the capable, loving hands of the God who formed you and knows you. Allow him to heal the wounds and brokenness that have tied you to the world, which you've been set free from through the death and resurrection of Jesus. Sanctification is ours by God's grace and mercy. Spend time in prayer allowing God to deal with your sin and lead you to a life of rejoicing and joy where only sin and sorrow dwelled before.

33

GUIDED PRAYER

1. Meditate on God's desire to produce holiness in you by his grace, love, and mercy.

"According to the foreknowledge of God the Father, in the sanctification of the Spirit, for obedience to Jesus Christ and for sprinkling with his blood: May grace and peace be multiplied to you." 1 Peter 1:2

"His divine power has granted to us all things that pertain to life and godliness, through the knowledge of him who called us to his own glory and excellence." 2 Peter 1:3

"And such were some of you. But you were washed, you were sanctified, you were justified in the name of the Lord Jesus Christ and by the Spirit of our God." 1 Corinthians 6:11

2. Open your life up to the Holy Spirit. Ask him to reveal areas that are keeping you from a life of holiness and godliness. Ask him to show you past wounds that are still hurting you today. Confess your sin to him and receive his forgiveness.

"If we confess our sins, he is faithful and just to forgive us our sins and to cleanse us from all unrighteousness." 1 John 1:9

"Whoever conceals his transgressions will not prosper, but he who confesses and forsakes them will obtain mercy." Proverbs 28:13

3. Now ask the Holy Spirit to come and heal you. Ask him to show you where he was at times when you were wounded. Ask him to reveal to you truth that has the power to cover the damaging lies the enemy has spoken to you. Live your life healed, set free, and delivered by the power of the Spirit.

"He himself bore our sins in his body on the tree, that we might die to sin and live to righteousness. By his wounds you have been healed." 1 Peter 2:24

May you experience the joy and freedom that comes from receiving God's forgiveness and healing. When we give our sins over to him and receive his forgiveness, the chains that entangled us to the cares of the world are shattered. Our portion in God is love, peace, and joy. Jesus died to set us free from the burden of sin. May you be a child of God marked by the holiness of your heavenly Father that is available in the Holy Spirit who dwells within you.

Extended Reading: 2 Peter 1

The Gifts of the Holy Spirit

DAY 7

DEVOTIONAL

Paul's heart for the Corinthians in 1 Corinthians 12:1 is God's heart for you and me today. Scripture says, *"Now concerning spiritual gifts, brothers, I do not want you to be uninformed."* Within the church today are defenders of multiple positions on spiritual gifts, each as staunch as the other. But God's desire for you and me is that we would be informed directly from him about the incredible gifts of this loving Holy Spirit who dwells within us. God longs for us to receive all he has to give. He longs to teach us about the Holy Spirit's work in our lives that we might live with greater purpose and affections for him and others. Let's surrender our hearts

and minds to God on spiritual gifts. And let's seek out every last bit of what God has planned for us today. The first aspect of spiritual gifts to note is that they are indeed a gift. 1 Corinthians 12:4-11 says,

Now there are varieties of gifts, but the same Spirit; and there are varieties of service, but the same Lord; and there are varieties of activities, but it is the same God who empowers them all in everyone. To each is given the manifestation of the Spirit for the common good. For to one is given through the Spirit the utterance of wisdom, and to another the utterance of knowledge according to

"Now concerning spiritual gifts, brothers, I do not want you to be uninformed."

1 CORINTHIANS 12:1

the same Spirit, to another faith by the same Spirit, to another gifts of healing by the one Spirit, to another the working of miracles, to another prophecy, to another the ability to distinguish between spirits, to another various kinds of tongues, to another the interpretation of tongues. All these are empowered by one and the same Spirit, who apportions to each one individually as he wills.

The Holy Spirit gives spiritual gifts to each of us. He *"apportions"* them according to his perfect wisdom. Spiritual gifts are never birthed by man and never given for selfish purposes. The Spirit gives us gifts because he loves us and others. All that he does is in perfect love and is for *"the common good."* Whether you've been given the gift of wisdom, knowledge, faith, healing, miracles, prophecy, discernment of spirits, tongues, or interpretation of tongues, your purpose in the gift is to be the same as the Holy Spirit's: love.

1 Corinthians 13:1-3 says, *"If I speak in the tongues of men and of angels, but have not love, I am a noisy gong or a clanging cymbal. And if I have prophetic powers, and understand all mysteries and all knowledge, and if I have all faith, so as to remove mountains, but have not love, I am nothing. If I give away all I have, and if I deliver up my body to be burned, but have not love, I gain nothing"* (emphasis added). Spiritual gifts are all about love. Operating in a gift of the Spirit is always to be done in love. Paul is clear that gifts are annoying (1 Corinthians 13:1) and worthless (1 Corinthians 13:2-3) if they are not filled with love.

1 Peter 4:10-11 says, *"As each has received a gift, use it to serve one another, as good stewards of God's varied grace: whoever speaks, as one who speaks oracles of God; whoever serves, as one who serves by the strength that God supplies—in order that in everything God may be glorified through Jesus Christ. To him belong glory and dominion forever and ever. Amen."* Spend time in prayer discovering what gift the Holy Spirit has given you and how he would intend you to use it for the benefit of the *"common good."* Choose to align your understanding and belief on spiritual gifts with the word of God alone. And live today operating in love with the amazing gifts God has given you, whatever they may be.

GUIDED PRAYER

1. Meditate on God's word about spiritual gifts. Align your understanding with his word alone.

"Now there are varieties of gifts, but the same Spirit; and there are varieties of service, but the same Lord; and there are varieties of activities, but it is the same God who empowers them all in everyone. To each is given the manifestation of the Spirit for the common good. For to one is given through the Spirit the utterance of wisdom, and to another the utterance of knowledge according to the same Spirit, to another faith by the same Spirit, to another gifts of healing by the one Spirit, to another the working of miracles, to another prophecy, to another the ability to distinguish between spirits, to another various kinds of tongues, to another the interpretation of tongues.

All these are empowered by one and the same Spirit, who apportions to each one individually as he wills."
1 Corinthians 12:4-11

2. Ask the Holy Spirit to reveal to you the gift he has given you. Ask him to show you if he's given you multiple gifts! Reflect on your life and the ways God has used you in the past. If you know someone who you believe has a close relationship with the Spirit, ask them what gift they believe God has given you!

3. Ask the Holy Spirit to use you today for the glory of Jesus. Decide to be a believer who lives empowered and purposed with the gift God has

given you. Ask the Spirit to show you ways he would use you. Stay in tune and ready to be used by the God of love today.

"As each has received a gift, use it to serve one another, as good stewards of God's varied grace: whoever speaks, as one who speaks oracles of God; whoever serves, as one who serves by the strength that God supplies—in order that in everything God may be glorified through Jesus Christ. To him belong glory and dominion forever and ever. Amen." 1 Peter 4:10-11

"Having gifts that differ according to the grace given to us, let us use them: if prophecy, in proportion to our faith; if service, in our serving; the one who teaches, in his teaching; the one who exhorts, in his exhortation; the one who contributes, in generosity; the one who leads, with zeal; the one who does acts of mercy, with cheerfulness." Romans 12:6-8

2 Timothy 1:6-7 says, *"For this reason I remind you to fan into flame the gift of God, which is in you through the laying on of my hands, for God gave us a spirit not of fear but of power and love and self-control."* Keep the fire of the Holy Spirit kindled within you today by intimate relationship with him. Talk with him. Ask for his help. Stay close to him and allow him to burn passionately within you to see the lost saved, loved, and freed.

Extended Reading: 1 Corinthians 12-14

God's manifest presence

"The Lord your God is in your midst." Zephaniah 3:17

WEEKLY OVERVIEW

God's presence is real, full of love, and completely transformational. It takes what was broken and brings healing. It takes what was lost and guides us to our rightful place in the Father. It satisfies the weary, brings light to the darkness, and pours out the refreshing rain of God's love on the driest, deepest parts of the soul. Scripture contains story after story of God coming down to meet God's children where they are, and your heavenly Father has the same heart for you as he did them. He longs to make the reality of his presence known to you. He longs to refresh you with his nearness. You were created for encountering God, and you will never be satisfied until you continually live in the experience for which you were created. Allow your desires to be stirred up to encounter the living God this week as we read powerful stories of God's people encountering his manifest presence. May you respond to God's word by seeking out that for which you were made: continual encounter with your heavenly Father.

The Reality of God's Presence

DAY 8

DEVOTIONAL

It's a troubling truth in Christianity today that many believers don't know about or aren't experiencing continual encounter with the real, manifest presence of God. The Bible contains story after story of life-changing, world-altering encounters with the reality of God's presence. From Moses and the tent of meeting to the disciples at Pentecost, we continually read about God supernaturally encountering his people in real, transformative ways. Jesus died so that we might walk in communion with our heavenly Father not only in heaven, but here on this earth. Biblical characters modeled what it was to experience God consistently in both the New and Old Testaments. God, in his desire to have restored relationship with you, has made the reality of his presence fully available to you. Through the death of Christ there is nothing separating you from him. Before we dive into different stories of God's manifest presence on the earth, let's take time to focus on the biblical basis for encountering God. Open your heart and mind to the truth about God's nearness and allow your faith to be stirred for all the ways your heavenly Father would transform your life through encounter with him.

Psalm 139:7-8 says, *"Where shall I go from your Spirit? Or where shall I flee from your presence? If I ascend to heaven, you are there! If I make my bed in Sheol, you are there!"* Acts 17:26-28 says,

And he made from one man every nation of mankind to live on all the face of the earth, having determined allotted periods and the boundaries of their dwelling place, that they should seek God, and perhaps feel their way toward him and find him. Yet he is actually not far from each one of us, for 'In him we live and move and have our being'; as even some of your own poets have said, 'For we are indeed his offspring.'

Scripture is clear that God is omnipresent and his presence can be tangible to us. David describes God's presence this way: *"In your presence there is fullness of joy; at your right hand are pleasures forevermore"* (Psalm 16:11).

"Where shall I go from your Spirit? Or where shall I flee from your presence? If I ascend to heaven, you are there! If I make my bed in Sheol, you are there!"

PSALM 139:7-8

The sons of Korah wrote in Psalm 84:1-2, *"How lovely is your dwelling place, O Lord of hosts! My soul longs, yes, faints for the courts of the Lord; my heart and flesh sing for joy to the living God."* Then in verses 10-12 they declare,

For a day in your courts is better than a thousand elsewhere. I would rather be a doorkeeper in the house of my God than dwell in the tents of wickedness. For the Lord God is a sun and shield; the Lord bestows favor and honor. No good thing does he withhold from those who walk uprightly. O Lord of hosts, blessed is the one who trusts in you!

There is no doubt in looking at Scripture that God's presence is real, good, and available to us. Rest in the truth of that for a moment. You can consistently enter into the tangible presence of your heavenly Father anywhere and anytime. Have faith today that God created you to experience him. Encountering his presence is made possible entirely by his grace, so it is available apart from any good or bad thing

you do. But, know that God will never force his presence on you. He only fills up what is open and ready to receive. He sweetly calls you to meet with him and waits for you to make space in your life to receive what he longs to give.

There is no more life-giving pursuit you can embark on than the pursuit of God's presence. Spending time resting in him is meant to be the satisfaction that lays a foundation for you to live the life of abundance made available to you through Jesus. Your role in encountering God is simply seeking him. If you will make time to encounter him, open your heart, and have faith in his word, then you will discover the wellspring of life, joy, love, and transformation that is the presence of our heavenly Father.

Deuteronomy 4:29 says, *"You will seek the Lord your God and you will find him, if you search after him with all your heart and with all your soul."* Seek and find the presence of the living God today as you meditate on his word and pray.

GUIDED PRAYER

1. Meditate on the availability of God's presence.

Allow your faith to be stirred up in response to God's word.

"The Lord is near to all who call on him, to all who call on him in truth." Psalm 145:18

"Where shall I go from your Spirit? Or where shall I flee from your presence? If I ascend to heaven, you are there! If I make my bed in Sheol, you are there!" Psalm 139:7-8

"And he made from one man every nation of mankind to live on all the face of the earth, having determined allotted periods and the boundaries of their dwelling place, that they should seek God, and perhaps feel their way toward him and find him. Yet he is actually not far from each one of us, for 'In him we live and move and have our being'; as even some of your own poets have said, 'For we are indeed his offspring.'" Acts 17:26-28

2. Now meditate on the goodness of God's presence.

Allow your desires to be stirred as you read about the wonders of encountering the living God.

"You make known to me the path of life; in your presence there is fullness of joy; at your right hand are pleasures forevermore." Psalm 16:11

"How lovely is your dwelling place, O Lord of hosts! My soul longs, yes, faints for the courts of the Lord; my heart and flesh sing for joy to the living God." Psalm 84:1-2

3. Open your heart to receive his presence.

Ask the Spirit to make known God's nearness. Seek his presence and have faith in his word that when you seek him you will find him.

"But from there you will seek the Lord your God and you will find him, if you search after him with all your heart and with all your soul." Deuteronomy 4:29

"And without faith it is impossible to please him, for whoever would draw near to God must believe that he exists and that he rewards those who seek him." Hebrews 11:6

In his book *The Knowledge of the Holy*, A.W. Tozer wrote, "With our loss of the sense of majesty has come the further loss of religious awe and consciousness of the divine Presence. We have lost our spirit of worship and our ability to withdraw inwardly to meet God in adoring silence." May his statement not be true of you. May you discover the majesty of your God. May you be a child of God who consistently spends time in the presence of the Father. May you be a believer who is empowered with the very presence of God himself working in and through your life. Grow in your pursuit of his presence this week. Commit to earnestly seeking him and allow this week to be transformational in the way you spend time with God.

Extended Reading: Psalm 84

48

Moses and the Tent of Meeting

DAY 9

DEVOTIONAL

Stories of Moses and the presence of God stir up my desire to meet with my heavenly Father face-to-face. We read in Exodus of God's faithfulness to lead, speak to, and encounter Moses. We read of Moses coming before his God boldly and asking for his hand in delivering and forgiving his people. Today, let's look at the story of Moses and the tent of meeting found in Exodus 33, and allow it to guide us into more consistent and impactful encounters with the living, all-powerful, and all-loving God.

Exodus 33:7-11 says,

Now Moses used to take the tent and pitch it outside the camp, far off from the camp, and he called it the tent of meeting. And everyone who sought the Lord would go out to the tent of meeting, which was outside the camp. Whenever Moses went out to the tent, all the people would rise up, and each would stand at his tent door, and watch Moses until he had gone into the tent. When Moses entered the tent, the pillar of cloud would descend and stand at the entrance of the tent, and the Lord would speak with Moses. And when all the people saw the pillar of cloud standing at the entrance of the tent, all the people would rise up and worship, each at his tent door. Thus the Lord used to speak to Moses face to face, as a man speaks to his friend. When Moses turned again into the camp, his assistant Joshua the son of Nun, a young man, would not depart from the tent.

Moses, a sinful, murdering, and fearful man, was able to see the living God *"face to face"* and speak with him *"as a man speaks to his friend."* Picture that tent in your mind's eye. Picture the cloud of God's presence descending from heaven in a way that everyone could see. Place yourself in that tent, hearing Moses talk with God, seeing the glory of God face-to-face with a broken, sinful man. What a picture of God's heart for us! If Moses could enter into the presence of God, surely all of us can. If Moses could speak with God face-to-face, surely we who have been bought with the blood of Christ can. If God would encounter Moses, speak to him, and guide him, he will surely do the same for each of us. In humility today, let's learn from this man who so faithfully encountered and followed God. Let's allow this story in Exodus to teach us how we might more fully and consistently meet with our heavenly Father.

The first thing we learn from this text is that Moses set up a place to meet consistently with God. It is crucially important that we find a place we can consistently seek the face of our heavenly Father. We need an uninterrupted time and place to rest in his presence in order to live our lives with his Spirit, word, and love as our foundation and fuel. Where can you meet with God consistently? What time in your day can be uninterrupted? The best time for me to meet with God is early in the morning before the rest of the world awakens to rush and busyness. When I don't

"Now Moses used to take the tent and pitch it outside the camp, far off from the camp, and he called it the tent of meeting. And everyone who sought the Lord would go out to the tent of meeting, which was outside the camp."

EXODUS 33:7

make time at the beginning of my morning to seek God's face, I scramble to find pockets of time throughout the day. And without this dedicated meeting with God, I have a much more difficult time living my life in light of the glorious goodness I can only discover in his tangible presence. Without consistently encountering my heavenly Father, I struggle to remain free from the burdens, lies, and sin that so easily entangle me though I have been set free by the blood of Jesus. May we be children of God who learn from Moses and make space and time in our lives to meet with our One, True Source of abundant life.

Next, we must believe that God longs to encounter us just as deeply as he longed to encounter Moses. God loves each of us to the absolute fullest extent possible. You are created for intimacy with your heavenly Father. There is no other path to the abundant life and destiny he has called you to than life lived in his presence. And there is no other way to live in step with his Spirit than spending time consistently encountering his presence. Hebrews 11:6 says, *"And without faith it is impossible to please him, for whoever would draw near to God must believe that he exists and that he rewards those who seek him."* God's greatest satisfaction is spending time with his children. His greatest joy is meeting with you face-to-face as he did with Moses. So great was his desire to encounter you that he offered up his only Son as payment for restored relationship. Believe in his desire to encoun-

ter you, believe that he will reward you when you seek him, and believe that you will discover a deeper reality of God's presence than you have ever encountered.

Lastly, know that as you encounter God consistently and abundantly, you will draw others to worship and seek a greater relationship with your heavenly Father. Exodus 33:10 says, *"And when all the people saw the pillar of cloud standing at the entrance of the tent, all the people would rise up and worship, each at his tent door."* We are designed to encounter the presence of God. We are made to see him face-to-face. So, living as God designed you—by consistently encountering his presence—will lead others to do the same. Others will see in you what they were created for and begin to pursue deeper relationships with God. The best way to lead others to God is out of consistent encounters with him. In encountering him, we naturally begin to become like him and therefore reveal his heart in all that we do.

May you be drawn into deeper encounters with your heavenly Father, whose love for you knows no bounds. Follow the example of Moses and find a consistent place to spend time seeking God's face. Have faith that God longs to encounter you and to make himself known to you. And as you spend time in his presence, may you naturally lead others to do the same.

Spend time in guided prayer allowing God to reveal himself fully to you.

GUIDED PRAYER

1. Meditate on how Moses met with God face-to-face and spoke with him. Allow God's word to stir your desires to meet directly with him as Moses did.

"When Moses entered the tent, the pillar of cloud would descend and stand at the entrance of the tent, and the Lord would speak with Moses." Exodus 33:9

"Thus the Lord used to speak to Moses face to face, as a man speaks to his friend." Exodus 33:11

2. Now seek the face of God in faith. Come before his throne boldly by the blood of Jesus. Believe that he loves you and longs to encounter you. And open your heart to receive all the love he would pour out on you in this moment.

"And without faith it is impossible to please him, for whoever would draw near to God must believe that he exists and that he rewards those who seek him." Hebrews 11:6

3. Rest in the presence of God. Spend time talking with him, receiving more of him, and being transformed by his nearness. Receive his love. Cast your burdens on him. Talk with him about anything that is weighing you down today.

"So that Christ may dwell in your hearts through faith—that you, being rooted and grounded in love, may have strength to comprehend with all the saints what is the breadth and length and height and depth, and to know the love of Christ that surpasses knowledge, that you may be filled with all the fullness of God." Ephesians 3:17-19

"Your steadfast love, O Lord, extends to the heavens, your faithfulness to the clouds." Psalm 36:5

"[Cast] all your anxieties on him, because he cares for you." 1 Peter 5:7

While we only see a glimpse of God here on earth, a glimpse of him is unequivocally better than any other sight. A glimpse of God is more powerful than a rushing wind, more real than your own skin, more vast than the oceans put together, and more satisfying than time spent with your closest friend. Whatever longing that feels unsatisfied can be quenched with a glimpse of your God. Run to his presence when you have need, or when you feel attacked or unfulfilled. Run to your tent of meeting when you need refreshment or guidance, or to talk with God. May you grow in your desire and ability to meet with your heavenly Father face-to-face, to talk with him and to be satisfied in his love.

Extended Reading: Exodus 34:29-35

DEVOTIONAL

Two of the most powerful recorded encounters of God's presence are found with Isaiah in Isaiah 6:1-7 and with Moses in Exodus 3:2-6. Let's open our hearts to both learn from these encounters and allow them to guide us into a powerful encounter with the living God ourselves.

Isaiah 6:1-7 says,

In the year that King Uzziah died I saw the Lord sitting upon a throne, high and lifted up; and the train of his robe filled the temple. Above him stood the seraphim. Each had six wings: with two he covered his face, and with two he covered his feet, and with two he flew. And one called to another and said:

"Holy, holy, holy is the Lord of hosts;
the whole earth is full of his glory!"

And the foundations of the thresholds shook at the voice of him who called, and the house was filled with smoke. And I said: "Woe is me! For I am lost; for I am a man of unclean lips, and I dwell in the midst of a people of unclean lips; for my eyes have seen the King, the Lord of hosts!"

Then one of the seraphim flew to me, having in his hand a burning coal that he had taken with tongs from the altar. And he touched my mouth and said: "Behold, this has touched your lips; your guilt is taken away, and your sin atoned for."

Isaiah demonstrated that experiencing the holiness of God and seeing our own sin in light of his holiness are consistent and important parts of encountering God's presence. Time after time in Scripture, God's people see their own sin, repent, and are healed after having an encounter with the presence of God. In fact, Moses has a similar response to being in the presence of God for the first time in Exodus 3:2-6:

And the angel of the Lord appeared to him in a flame of fire out of the midst of a bush. He looked, and behold, the bush was burning, yet it was not consumed. And

> *"And the angel of the Lord appeared to him in a flame of fire out of the midst of a bush. He looked, and behold, the bush was burning, yet it was not consumed."*
>
> **EXODUS 3:2**

Moses said, "I will turn aside to see this great sight, why the bush is not burned." When the Lord saw that he turned aside to see, God called to him out of the bush, "Moses, Moses!" And he said, "Here I am." Then he said, "Do not come near; take your sandals off your feet, for the place on which you are standing is holy ground." And he said, "I am the God of your father, the God of Abraham, the God of Isaac, and the God of Jacob." And Moses hid his face, for he was afraid to look at God.

In light of God's astounding holiness, Moses was filled with fear to look at the face of God. These two descriptions of God's presence illustrate an important truth for all: the light of God's holiness has the ability to pierce into the depth of our soul, bringing to light the darkness that destroys us from within. My prayer today is that we would follow the examples of Moses and Isaiah and allow God's holiness to shine light on our sin and draw us to repentance. And may we experience healing today the way Isaiah did as the angel of the Lord cleansed him with the coal.

God's presence casts light on our sin and brokenness because in order for us to live the fullness of life God desires, we must walk in righteousness. It's because of God's love that he reveals our sin. It's because God longs for us to experience a life of holiness and freedom as his children that he shines light on our darkness and draws us out into the glorious light of righteousness.

God promises in Isaiah 42:16, *"And I will lead the blind in a way that they do not know, in paths that they have not known I will guide them. I will turn the darkness before them into light, the rough places into level ground. These are the things I do, and I do not forsake them."* And 1 Peter 2:9 says, *"But you are a chosen race, a royal priesthood, a holy nation, a people for his own possession, that you may proclaim the excellencies of him who called you out of darkness into his marvelous light."* God's desire has always been to lead his children into his righteousness. God's longing for us to partake in his divine nature has been a chief desire of his from the first sin of Adam and Eve. And through the life, death, and resurrection of Christ our nature has been transformed. Ephesians 2:1-6 says,

And you were dead in the trespasses and sins in which you once walked, following the course of this world, following the prince of the power of the air, the spirit that is now at work in the sons of disobedience— among whom we all once lived in the passions of our flesh, carrying out the desires of the body and the mind, and were by nature children of wrath, like the rest of mankind. But God, being rich in mercy, because of the great love with which he loved us, even when we were dead in our trespasses, made us alive together with Christ—by grace you have been saved— and raised us up with him and seated us with him in the heavenly places in Christ Jesus.

You have been set free from what once separated you from your heavenly Father. But the key to experiencing this freedom is allowing God to shine light on what does not belong to you anymore: your

sin. You must walk as a child of the light, not as a child of wrath, and it's spending time encountering the holiness of God that will transform you from the inside out. Spending time on holy ground as Moses did will heal you from the sins that entangle you. Spending time allowing God to reveal your sin and purge it from you as he did with Isaiah will empower you to choose the light over the darkness. A vital part of encountering God is repenting of our sin in light of his wonderful, holy love for us.

Experience the holiness of God today as you enter into guided prayer. Repent of whatever is in you that's not in line with your new nature in Christ and walk as the child of God that you are in light of his wonderful and powerful grace.

GUIDED PRAYER

1. Meditate on Moses and Isaiah's encounters with the holiness of God. Put yourself inside the story. Imagine yourself as their character. Feel what they would have felt. See what they would have seen. Allow the stories of Scripture to come to life around you.

2. Allow the holiness of God to shine light on the darkest parts of your soul. Where do you have unconfessed sin? What's holding you back from walking fully in the light? What sin does God want to heal you from today?

3. Confess your sins to God. Repent from any area of darkness and turn fully toward the light of holiness. Rest in his forgiveness and allow it to be the foundation on which you can live in the freedom bought for you by the blood of Christ.

Psalm 30:11 says, *"You have turned for me my mourning into dancing; you have loosed my sackcloth and clothed me with gladness."* When we give our sin over to God he turns what the enemy meant to harm us into our greatest source of gladness. Forgiveness is something to dance over, to sing about, and to enjoy wholeheartedly. Our God takes what was dark and makes it light. He took what tied us to this world, placed it on the shoulders of Jesus, and put it to death with the last breath of his perfect Son. May you discover today a freeing joy in the presence of the God of holiness and forgiveness. And may you live your life in light of the glorious grace you've been shown through the love of God.

Extended Reading: Romans 8

The Pillar of God's Presence

DEVOTIONAL

One of the greatest realities of God's presence is the way it guides us. Exodus 13:21-22 provides an illustration for an important truth God would have us know today: when we need guidance we can run to his presence and discover his leadership in abundance. Scripture tells us, *"And the Lord went before them by day in a pillar of cloud to lead them along the way, and by night in a pillar of fire to give them light, that they might travel by day and by night. The pillar of cloud by day and the pillar of fire by night did not depart from before the people."*

Even in the Israelites' sin, God faithfully led them. Even in their lack of faith, he still provided miraculous leadership. And now, through believing in the death and resurrection of Jesus, we have been filled with the presence of God himself. We've been given the miraculous gift of the Holy Spirit who is always present with us and in us. As amazing as it is that God led his people with pillars of cloud and fire, how much more

presence of God by the work of Christ? Jesus made a way for us to know the will of God with every moment as we fellowship with the Spirit of God himself.

So, how can we follow the Spirit as the Israelites followed the pillars of fire and cloud? How can we discover the abundance of leadership available to us through the presence of God? First, we must acknowledge our need of his leadership and seek out his counsel. He can only guide those who choose to follow. If you choose to go your own way in life you will step outside the guidance of his presence. It's in seeking his will that we discover the vast reservoir of the Spirit's perfect leadership. Proverbs 3:5-6 says, *"Trust in the Lord with all your heart, and do not lean on your own understanding. In all your ways acknowledge him, and he will make straight your paths."* Acknowledge him. Acknowledge the reality of his presence in your life in all your ways. Trust in his guidance rather than your own understanding,

"And the Lord went before them by day in a pillar of cloud to lead them along the way, and by night in a pillar of fire to give them light, that they might travel by day and by night. The pillar of cloud by day and the pillar of fire by night did not depart from before the people."

EXODUS 13:21-22

Second, you have to believe that God can and will guide you when you ask for his leadership. Isaiah 58:11 says, *"And the Lord will guide you continually and satisfy your desire in scorched places and make your bones strong; and you shall be like a watered garden, like a spring of water, whose waters do not fail."* This world is suffering from a lack of God's guidance. We live in a world continuously searching, striving, and yearning for some sort of message of leadership. All around us the blind lead the blind into greater depths of darkness, continually searching for what we have already found in God. God longs to satisfy your desire for leadership. He longs to make you *"like a watered garden, like a spring of water, whose waters do not fail."* All you have to do is ask him. James 1:5 says, *"If any of you lacks wisdom, let him ask God, who gives generously to all without reproach, and it will be given him."* God will guide you when you seek him for wisdom. He will lead you to the perfect will he has for you if you humble yourself before him and commit to following him. All you have to do is ask and follow the Spirit's guidance in however he chooses to lead you. He will make his leadership clear if you stay behind him and listen.

Last, you must follow his leadership to experience the fruit of his guiding presence. The prize of a winning lottery ticket remains worthless until it is cashed in. The contents of a gift remain useless until it is opened. You have been given the most incredible gift of all: God's guiding presence in your life. Proverbs 3:13-18 says,

Blessed is the one who finds wisdom, and the one who gets understanding, for the gain from her is better than gain from silver and her profit better than gold. She is more precious than jewels, and nothing you desire can compare with her. Long life is in her right hand; in her left hand are riches and honor. Her ways are ways of pleasantness, and all her paths are peace. She is a tree of life to those who lay hold of her; those who hold her fast are called blessed.

But until you choose to follow the wisdom of God in your life, you won't experience an ounce of its value. Until you follow the wise guidance of the Holy Spirit, you won't experience the incredible, abundant life he has in store for you. James 1:22-25 commands us,

But be doers of the word, and not hearers only, deceiving yourselves. For if anyone is a hearer of the word and not a doer, he is like a man who looks intently at his natural face in a mirror. For he looks at himself and goes away and at once forgets what he was like. But the one who looks into the perfect law, the law of liberty, and perseveres, being no hearer who forgets but a doer who acts, he will be blessed in his doing.

Persevere today in God's presence. Seek out his wisdom and counsel during guided prayer. Lay the burden of leading your own life on his mighty and loving shoulders, and allow the Holy Spirit to guide you into the abundant life he has prepared for you.

GUIDED PRAYER

1. Meditate on God's desire and ability to lead you.

"And the Lord went before them by day in a pillar of cloud to lead them along the way, and by night in a pillar of fire to give them light, that they might travel by day and by night. The pillar of cloud by day and the pillar of fire by night did not depart from before the people." Exodus 13:21-22

"And the Lord will guide you continually and satisfy your desire in scorched places and make your bones strong; and you shall be like a watered garden, like a spring of water, whose waters do not fail." Isaiah 58:11

"Call to me and I will answer you, and will tell you great and hidden things that you have not known." Jeremiah 33:3

2. Now meditate on the value of God's leadership in your life.
Trust in his word. Believe that his wisdom is far greater than your own. Trust in Scripture that what he leads you to is far beyond anything you could discover yourself.

"Blessed is the one who finds wisdom, and the one who gets understanding, for the gain from her is better than gain from silver and her profit better than gold. She is more precious than jewels, and nothing you desire can compare with her. Long life is in her right hand; in her left hand are riches and honor. Her ways are ways of pleasantness, and all her paths are peace. She is a tree of life to those who lay hold of her; those who hold her fast are called blessed." Proverbs 3:13-18

"And the Lord will guide you continually and satisfy your desire in scorched places and make your bones strong; and you shall be like a watered garden, like a spring of water, whose waters do not fail." Isaiah 58:11

3. Now ask the Spirit for wisdom and guidance in your life.
Where do you need the mind of Christ today? What issue before you do you not know how to handle well? Where do you need the leadership of God? Lay your questions at his feet, and pay attention to how he responds to you. Wait for an answer in his presence and continue to look for his responses throughout your day. Trust that he will guide you perfectly into every good thing he has for you.

"Trust in the Lord with all your heart, and do not lean on your own understanding. In all your ways acknowledge him, and he will make straight your paths." Proverbs 3:5-6

"If any of you lacks wisdom, let him ask God, who gives generously to all without reproach, and it will be given him." James 1:5

The prayer of Paul to the Ephesians is my prayer for you today. May you be blessed with the vast reservoir of God's wonderful guidance:

"I do not cease to give thanks for you, remembering you in my prayers, that the God of our Lord Jesus Christ, the Father of glory, may give you a spirit of wisdom and of revelation in the knowledge of him, having the eyes of your hearts enlightened, that you may know what is the hope to which he has called you, what are the riches of his glorious inheritance in the saints, and what is the immeasurable greatness of his power toward us who believe, according to the working of his great might." Ephesians 1:16-19

Extended Reading: Proverbs 3

The Holy of Holies

SCRIPTURE

"Therefore, brothers, since we have confidence to enter the holy places by the blood of Jesus, by the new and living way that he opened for us through the curtain, that is, through his flesh, and since we have a great priest over the house of God, let us draw near with a true heart in full assurance of faith, with our hearts sprinkled clean from an evil conscience and our bodies washed with pure water." Hebrews 10:19-22

DEVOTIONAL

Descriptions of the Holy of Holies strike fear in my heart. Leviticus 16:1-5 describes the work a priest would have to go through in order to enter into the presence of God and not be killed. Scripture says,

The Lord spoke to Moses after the death of the two sons of Aaron, when they drew near before the Lord and died, and the Lord said to Moses, "Tell Aaron your brother not to come at any time into the Holy Place inside the veil, before the mercy seat that is on the ark, so that he may not die. For I will appear in the cloud over the mercy seat. But in this way Aaron shall come into the Holy Place: with a bull from the herd for a sin offering and a ram for a burnt offering. He shall put on the holy linen coat and shall have the linen undergarment on his body, and he shall tie the linen sash around his waist, and wear the linen turban; these are the holy garments. He shall bathe his body in water and then put them on. And he shall take from the congregation of the people of Israel two male goats for a sin offering, and one ram for a burnt offering."

The holiness of God required absolute purity from all who would enter into his presence. And so powerful was God's presence that it killed the two sons of Aaron, the high priest. When I picture the terrifying, powerful presence of my God as told in the Old Testament, my heart is filled with reverence and awe. How could this holy God love me, a broken and helpless sinner? How could I come before God and enter into his presence when his holiness requires such purity?

But Hebrews 9:11-12 says,

When Christ appeared as a high priest of the good things that have come, then through the greater and more perfect tent (not made with hands, that is, not of this creation) he entered once for all into the holy places, not by means of the blood of goats and calves but by means of his own blood, thus securing an eternal redemption.

Our high priest entered into the holy places on our behalf and secured safe passage for us all to enter into God's presence. Hebrews 10:19-22 describes this powerful truth in saying,

Therefore, brothers, since we have confidence to enter the holy places by the blood of Jesus, by the new and living way that he opened for us through the curtain, that is, through his flesh, and since we have a great priest over the house of God, let us draw near with a true heart in full assurance of faith, with our hearts sprinkled clean from an evil conscience and our bodies washed with pure water.

What's more, through the death of Jesus, God is now able to flood the earth with his presence. Christ defeated the power of sin and death and made the way for you and me to be the new temple of God's holy, powerful presence. 1 Corinthians 3:16-17 states, *"Do you not know that you are God's temple and that God's Spirit dwells in you? If anyone destroys God's temple, God will destroy him. For God's temple is holy, and you are that temple."* Later, 1 Corinthians 6:19-20 says, *"Or do you not know that your body is a temple of the Holy Spirit within you, whom you have from God? You are not your own, for you were bought with a price. So glorify God in your body."*

The question before you today is this: are you experiencing the fullness of what has been made available to you through Christ? Are you experiencing the power and nearness of the God who has made his temple within you? Are you living out of the holiness of the very Spirit who dwells within you and has made you a righteous new creation (2 Corinthians 5:17, 2 Corinthians 5:21)?

1 Corinthians 6:20 commands us to *"glorify God in [our] body"* as a response to being filled with the presence of God through the work of our high priest, Jesus Christ. It's in living our life out of the inner working of the Holy Spirit that we begin to experience all that God intends for us. We must first acknowledge that the very presence of God who dwelled within the Holy of Holies and was so powerful that it killed men now dwells within us. The same Spirit who raised Christ from the dead lives within us. And in acknowledging the reality of God's presence in our lives we must begin to realign our lives with the will of the Spirit. We must react to God's grace with our obedience. So great was God's desire to provide you with an abundant life in him that he sent Jesus as the final, perfect sacrifice. The fact that you are now the temple of the Holy Spirit means that you have God himself to guide you, love you, fill you, heal you, and deliver you. You have access to a more real and intimate relationship with your heavenly Father than you can fathom.

Spend time in prayer acknowledging the presence of God within you and responding to his presence with humility and trust. Allow the Spirit to transform you in his presence and guide you into who you were created to be. May you encounter the power of the God who loves you too much to allow you to lead a life apart from his holy and loving presence.

63

GUIDED PRAYER

1. Meditate on the power of the presence of God that dwells within you. Reflect on the holiness of God as described in the Old Testament accounts of the Holy of Holies.

"The Lord spoke to Moses after the death of the two sons of Aaron, when they drew near before the Lord and died, and the Lord said to Moses, 'Tell Aaron your brother not to come at any time into the Holy Place inside the veil, before the mercy seat that is on the ark, so that he may not die. For I will appear in the cloud over the mercy seat. But in this way Aaron shall come into the Holy Place: with a bull from the herd for a sin offering and a ram for a burnt offering. He shall put on the holy linen coat and shall have the linen undergarment on his body, and he shall tie the linen sash around his waist, and wear the linen turban; these are the holy garments. He shall bathe his body in water and then put them on. And he shall take from the congregation of the people of Israel two male goats for a sin offering, and one ram for a burnt offering.'" Leviticus 16:1-5

"On its hem you shall make pomegranates of blue and purple and scarlet yarns, around its hem, with bells of gold between them, a golden bell and a pomegranate, a golden bell and a pomegranate, around the hem of the robe. And it shall be on Aaron when he ministers, and its sound shall be heard when he goes into the Holy Place before the Lord, and when he comes out, so that he does not die." Exodus 28:33-35

2. Now meditate on the fact that you are the temple of the Holy Spirit. Acknowledge the reality of the Holy Spirit in your life. Open your heart and mind to experience his nearness, love, and power.

"Do you not know that you are God's temple and that God's Spirit dwells in you? If anyone destroys God's temple, God will destroy him. For God's temple is holy, and you are that temple." 1 Corinthians 3:16-17

"Or do you not know that your body is a temple of the Holy Spirit within you, whom you have from God? You are not your own, for you were bought with a price. So glorify God in your body." 1 Corinthians 6:19-20

3. Come before God with the boldness made available to you through Christ. Ask the Spirit to guide you deeper into God's presence. Ask God to reveal to you new parts of his love for you. God is infinite. His presence never runs out. Take time to rest in the wonderful, real, and loving presence of your heavenly Father.

"But when Christ appeared as a high priest of the good things that have come, then through the greater and more perfect tent (not made with hands, that is, not of this creation) he entered once for all into the holy places, not by means of the blood of goats and calves but by means of his own blood, thus securing an eternal redemption." Hebrews 9:11-12

"Therefore, brothers, since we have confidence to enter the holy places by the blood of Jesus, by the new and living way that he opened for us through the curtain, that is, through his flesh, and since we have a great priest over the house of God, let us draw near with a true heart in full assurance of faith, with our hearts sprinkled clean from an evil conscience and our bodies washed with pure water." Hebrews 10:19-22

In God's presence you can experience all he longs to do in you. Allow the Spirit to guide you to past wounds that need to be healed. If you are suffering from a physical ailment, ask the Spirit to heal you. God's Spirit is as alive and active today as ever, working to heal the brokenness of a world wrought with the destruction of sin. Allow him to work in you, that you might be a picture to others of the reality of your heavenly Father's love for his children. Open your heart, ask him to move and work, and receive whatever it is he desires to give you today. There's no time like being in the presence of God to experience all that he has to offer us in his love and grace.

Extended Reading: Hebrews 9-10

Pentecost

DAY 13

SCRIPTURE

"When the day of Pentecost arrived, they were all together in one place. And suddenly there came from heaven a sound like a mighty rushing wind, and it filled the entire house where they were sitting." Acts 2:1-2

DEVOTIONAL

Pentecost marks the powerful beginning of a global movement of the power of God's presence sweeping across the earth. As we read the account of what happened as the Spirit descended with power on God's people, place yourself in their midst. Imagine what it would look like, sound like, and feel like to witness firsthand such a powerful movement of God's Spirit:

When the day of Pentecost arrived, they were all together in one place. And suddenly there came from heaven a sound like a mighty rushing wind, and it filled the entire house where they were sitting. And divided tongues as of fire appeared to them and rested on each one of them. And they were all filled with the Holy Spirit and began to speak in other tongues as the Spirit gave them utterance.

Now there were dwelling in Jerusalem Jews, devout men from every nation under heaven. And at this sound the multitude came together, and they were bewildered, because each one was hearing them speak in his own language. And they were amazed and astonished, saying, "Are not all these who are speaking Galileans? And how is it that we hear, each of us in his own native language?

Parthians and Medes and Elamites and residents of Mesopotamia, Judea and Cappadocia, Pontus and Asia, Phrygia and Pamphylia, Egypt and the parts of Libya belonging to Cyrene, and visitors from Rome, both Jews and proselytes, Cretans and Arabians—we hear them telling in our own tongues the mighty works of God." And all were amazed and perplexed, saying to one another, "What does this mean?" But others mocking said, "They are filled with new wine" (Acts 2:1-13).

The Holy Spirit is our greatest gift. When the disciples received the Spirit they began living as Jesus did. They began speaking to, healing, and transforming a world that had known no restored relationship with their Creator since Adam and Eve. And Scripture makes it clear that our lives are to follow their example. We've been given the same Spirit as the disciples, who moved so powerfully in revealing our loving heavenly Father to a world in desperate need of relationship with their Creator. I feel that there are three areas in which the Spirit would anoint us more powerfully today as he did the disciples at Pentecost. Let's boldly seek out all that the Spirit would do in our hearts and lives today.

The first act of the disciples upon being filled with the Spirit at Pentecost was to speak to all who would listen, explaining all the powerful acts that were going on around them. And with the preaching of Peter three thousand listeners accepted the free gift of salvation.

We who are marked by the Spirit's presence are to be disciples who move in the power of love. Acts 1:8 says, *"But you will receive power when the Holy Spirit has come upon you, and you will be my witnesses in Jerusalem and in all Judea and Samaria, and to the end of the earth."* The Spirit longs to use us to proclaim the goodness of God's love to this lost and dying world. He longs to fill us with the desire to love this world the way he does. 1 Corinthians 16:14 says, *"Let all that you do be done in love."* Galatians 5:22 says, *"But the fruit of the Spirit is love."* And in Mark 12:31, Jesus says that the second greatest commandment is, *"You shall love your neighbor as yourself."* Is your life marked by love for others? Do you live your life in service to your heavenly Father and his children? Seek out a fresh encounter with the Holy Spirit today. It's the Spirit who bears the fruit of love in your life. You cannot love others on your own, for true love comes solely from God. But, the Spirit longs to fill you with a desire and anointing to love others around you that they might better know the love of the heavenly Father.

The coming of the Holy Spirit also brought powerful unity to the disciples. Acts 2:44-47 says,

And all who believed were together and had all things in common. And they were selling their possessions and belongings and distributing the proceeds to all, as any had need. And day by day, attending the temple together and breaking bread in their homes, they received their food with glad and generous hearts, praising God and having favor with all the people. And the Lord added to their number day by day those who were being saved.

Only the Spirit can bring unity between broken, competitive, and needy people. Only through the Spirit do we have the ability to love and accept others regardless of our differences and unite toward the common goal of loving God and others wholeheartedly. Paul writes in Ephesians 4:1-3, *"I therefore, a prisoner for the Lord, urge you to walk in a manner worthy of the calling to which you have been called, with all humility and gentleness, with patience, bearing with one another in love, eager to maintain the unity of the Spirit in the bond of peace."* Are you a disciple marked by a desire to *"maintain the unity of the Spirit in the bond of peace?"* Are you a Christian marked by grace-filled love for your fellow believers? We all need to seek out greater anointing and desire from the Spirit toward unity. We cannot be selfless in our own strength. We need the help of the God of perfect love to pursue unity through humility. Seek out a desire and anointing to be a person who works toward the goal of unity instead of division today. Spend time in God's presence allowing him to transform your heart to look more like his.

Lastly, Pentecost filled the disciples with the ability to connect directly to God through the avenue of the Holy Spirit. Paul writes in 1 Corinthians 2:10, *"These things God has revealed to us through the Spirit. For the Spirit searches everything, even the depths of God."* Acts 15:28 says, *"For it has seemed good to the Holy Spirit and to us to lay on you no greater burden than these requirements."* The disciples knew God's desires, received revelation from him, and were transformed into the likeness of Christ through fellowshipping with the Holy Spirit. We as disciples are to be marked by direct connection with the Holy Spirit. Paul and Peter had no special human ability to talk to God. Prior to the coming of the Holy Spirit, Paul was killing children of the very God he was trying to serve, and Peter chose his own safety over Jesus, who had shown him such immense love and grace. It was only with the Holy Spirit that these men were able to connect to God so deeply, and we can have that same connection today. So, are you a believer marked by direct connection with the Holy Spirit? Do you spend time seeking his presence, counsel, and anointing? Let's be children of God who pursue deeper connection with our heavenly Father today. Let's seek the face of God as the early disciples did and be believers marked by relationship with the Holy Spirit.

Spend time during guided prayer pursuing all that the Spirit would do in you. Open your heart and mind to be transformed by his love. And commit to living your life with direct connection to the God who dwells within you.

GUIDED PRAYER

1. Meditate on the Spirit's desire and ability to anoint us with the power and desire to love others. Ask him to show you how to better love others today. Ask his forgiveness for any way in which you have been hurtful to those whom he loves. And receive the anointing to love people from his heart and strength rather than your own.

"But you will receive power when the Holy Spirit has come upon you, and you will be my witnesses in Jerusalem and in all Judea and Samaria, and to the end of the earth." Acts 1:8

"Let all that you do be done in love." 1 Corinthians 16:14

"You shall love your neighbor as yourself." Mark 12:31

2. Now meditate on God's desire to use you to bring unity to his children. Confess to God anyone who annoys you or angers you. Confess anyone whom you have a hard time loving. Ask him for his heart for that person. Ask him to fill you up with a supernatural ability to love those who are difficult or different. Ask him to help you be a person who pursues unity.

"And all who believed were together and had all things in common. And they were selling their possessions and belongings and distributing the proceeds to all, as any had need. And day by day, attending the temple together and breaking bread in their homes, they received their food with glad and generous hearts, praising God and having favor with all the people. And the Lord added to their number day by day those who were being saved." Acts 2:44-47

"I therefore, a prisoner for the Lord, urge you to walk in a manner worthy of the calling to which you have been called, with all humility and gentleness, with patience, bearing with one another in love, eager to maintain the unity of the Spirit in the bond of peace." Ephesians 4:1-3

3. Now seek after a direct connection to the Holy Spirit. Ask him to guide you into the knowledge of his presence. Ask him to show you the overwhelming love, grace, and anointing he has for you today. Seek out answers to any questions you have of him. May you discover a wellspring of friendship in the Holy Spirit today.

"But for me it is good to be near God; I have made the Lord God my refuge, that I may tell of all your works." Psalm 73:28

"These things God has revealed to us through the Spirit. For the Spirit searches everything, even the depths of God." 1 Corinthians 2:10

"And we impart this in words not taught by human wisdom but taught by the Spirit, interpreting spiritual truths to those who are spiritual." 1 Corinthians 2:13

It's crucial that we as children of God seek out all that he longs to give us. Relationship with God is meant to be anything but stale, stagnant, and weak. The disciples demonstrated that those filled with the Spirit of God are to be marked by adventure, mystery, and the miraculous. God has a story for the ages written with you in mind. He has a plan beyond what you could ever imagine if you will seek him out, trust him, and follow him. Rest today in the fact that God loves you enough to lead you away from a mundane life. Pursue his plans and watch as he fills your life with adventure and wonder.

Extended Reading: Acts 2

The Baptism
of Jesus

DAY 14

DEVOTIONAL

The baptism of Jesus lays the foundation on which you and I can return time and time again to experience the abundant life made available to us at salvation. Matthew 3:16-17 says, *"And when Jesus was baptized, immediately he went up from the water, and behold, the heavens were opened to him, and he saw the Spirit of God descending like a dove and coming to rest on him; and behold, a voice from heaven said, 'This is my beloved Son, with whom I am well pleased.'"* Through the baptism of Jesus the Spirit of God powerfully enters into the scene of humanity. The Holy Spirit's always been moving and working, but through Christ the way was paved for him to fill us and rest on us. Through the baptism of Jesus, we can all be baptized with the Spirit (John 1:33, John 3:5).

Peter says in Acts 2:38, *"Repent and be baptized every one of you in the name of Jesus Christ for the forgiveness of your sins, and you will receive the gift of the Holy Spirit."* And Romans 6:4 tells us, *"We were buried*

"And when Jesus was baptized, immediately he went up from the water, and behold, the heavens were opened to him, and he saw the Spirit of God descending like a dove and coming to rest on him; and behold, a voice from heaven said, 'This is my beloved Son, with whom I am well pleased.'"

MATTHEW 3:16-17

therefore with him by baptism into death, in order that, just as Christ was raised from the dead by the glory of the Father, we too might walk in newness of life." At salvation the Spirit descends on us and fills us. He is the promise of God for our eternal life. He is our Helper, Teacher, and Comforter while we are here on earth. And he is the one who leads us into the abundant, new life made available to us through Christ.

You see, just as the Spirit rested on Jesus, through his presence in our lives we have untapped resources of unconditional rest. God desires that we would rest in him as he rests on us. He desires for his children to find the only consistent source of peace available to us through the presence of the Holy Spirit in our lives. Where do you need rest today? What trouble, situation, thought, or person is stealing your peace? The Holy Spirit wants to descend on you today as he did on Jesus. He wants to guide you into the rest of your heavenly Father. Isaiah 40:28-31 says,

The Lord is the everlasting God, the Creator of the ends of the earth. He does not faint or grow weary; his understanding is unsearchable. He gives power to the faint, and to him who has no might he increases strength. Even youths shall faint and be weary, and young men shall fall exhausted; but they who wait for the Lord shall renew their strength; they shall mount up with wings like eagles; they shall run and not be weary; they shall walk and not faint.

You have the one who never faints or tires and gives power and might dwelling within you as a follower of Jesus. You have an inexhaustible resource of joy, strength, renewal, and rest readily available to you in the Spirit. All that is required of you is to make space in your life to enter into the rest God longs to provide you. Allow him to lay a foundation of his presence in your life by spending time simply being with him, and he will transform you into a person of the Spirit who fellowships and receives from the Spirit constantly. Learn to listen to his voice, follow his guidance, and enjoy his presence today.

Wherever you need rest today the Holy Spirit is waiting to provide it for you. As you pray, make space in your heart and day to rest in him as he rests on you.

71

GUIDED PRAYER

1. Meditate on the Spirit's desire to descend on you as he did on Jesus. Allow your faith to be stirred to have a real, tangible encounter with the Holy Spirit.

"And when Jesus was baptized, immediately he went up from the water, and behold, the heavens were opened to him, and he saw the Spirit of God descending like a dove and coming to rest on him; and behold, a voice from heaven said, 'This is my beloved Son, with whom I am well pleased.'" Matthew 3:16-17

"I myself did not know him, but he who sent me to baptize with water said to me, 'He on whom you see the Spirit descend and remain, this is he who baptizes with the Holy Spirit.'" John 1:33

2. Reflect on your own life. Where in your life do you need rest today? Where do you need a fresh encounter with the Holy Spirit? What trouble seems to plague you? What brokenness needs healing and peace?

3. Ask the Spirit to descend on you and bring you rest. Ask for him to make his presence a reality to you. Follow him as he guides you into his presence. Worship, pray, and read the word. Do whatever will guide you into an encounter with the presence of God. God longs to bring you rest. It's his desire that brings his presence, not your ability to feel him. He makes himself known when we open up our hearts and wait on him. Spend time waiting on his presence and resting in his love.

"And he said, 'My presence will go with you, and I will give you rest.'" Exodus 33:14

"The Lord is the everlasting God, the Creator of the ends of the earth. He does not faint or grow weary; his understanding is unsearchable. He gives power to the faint, and to him who has no might he increases strength. Even youths shall faint and be weary, and young men shall fall exhausted; but they who wait for the Lord shall renew their strength; they shall mount up with wings like eagles; they shall run and not be weary; they shall walk and not faint." Isaiah 40:28-31

"For I will satisfy the weary soul, and every languishing soul I will replenish." Jeremiah 31:25

May you discover today the path to continual encounter with the Holy Spirit. He isn't a God who separates himself into different sections of your life. You are created to live in continual, tangible relationship with your heavenly Father. You are created to find consistent rest in his loving presence. When you begin to feel the burdens of the world weighing you down and robbing you of the abundant life that is yours in Christ, take a minute and receive his presence again. Find consistent times throughout your day to press into the heart of God and discover his continual, new, and refreshing presence that's available to you anytime and anyplace. Don't allow a mediocre day to be enough today. Press into the Spirit for more and find all that God intended for your life.

Extended Reading: Isaiah 40

Experiencing God

*"You will seek me and find me.
when you seek me with all your
heart." Jeremiah 29:13*

WEEKLY OVERVIEW

To know God is to experience God. Just as we experience aspects of one another as we grow in friendship, we experience the wonders of God as we seek to simply know him. God is calling us to a life of seeking him with all we are. He is calling us to value relationship with him above all else that we would love no other but him. May you encounter wonderful aspects of relationship with your heavenly Father this week as we wholeheartedly seek to know him with all we are.

God Wants to be Known

DEVOTIONAL

The single greatest privilege in life is to know God. The God who formed you, provides for you and sent his Son to die for you longs to have real relationship with you. He longs to be known by you. And through the powerful sacrifice of Jesus, we truly can know him like any other person. And in fact, in some respects he is infinitely more knowable than any other person. Jeremiah 31:33-34 says,

*"Be still, and know that I am God. I
will be exalted among the nations, I
will be exalted in the earth!"*

PSALM 46:10

*But this is the covenant that I will make with the house
of Israel after those days, declares the Lord: I will put
my law within them, and I will write it on their hearts.
And I will be their God, and they shall be my people.
And no longer shall each one teach his neighbor and
each his brother, saying, "Know the Lord," for they
shall all know me, from the least of them to the greatest,
declares the Lord. For I will forgive their iniquity, and
I will remember their sin no more.*

"From the least of them to the greatest," says the living
God. No matter who you are, no matter what you've
done, you can know the God of love. Knowing God
is no longer reserved for those individually appointed
as his leaders. Knowing God is no longer reserved
for those like David, Isaiah, Peter, or the clergy. All of
us have equal access to the living God.

And from the place of knowing God, we are granted
the ability to experience his incredible attributes and
be blessed by a greater awareness of our union with
him. When we seek to know God, the Bible is clear
that we begin to experience his love (Romans 5:5),
hear his voice (John 10:27), and feel his peace (2
Thessalonians 3:16). We can partner in his purposes
(1 Peter 2:9), experience his freedom (Romans 6:4),
and rest in his presence (Psalm 16:11).

When we center our lives around knowing God,
we gain experience with him like we do any other
person. I don't seek to hear my wife's voice, rather
I seek to know her and have conversation with
her as a byproduct of that. I don't seek just the
emotion of love from my wife; rather, in getting
to know her and walking in relationship with her,
I experience her affections for me. So it is with
God. When we simply seek to know him we gain
experience in return.

I pray that as we look at the individual aspects of
experiencing God this week your heart is stirred
to simply seek deeper relationship with your
heavenly Father, whatever may come as the result.
Your Father loves you enough to pay the ultimate
price to have relationship with you. Seek him and
discover the wealth of his affections for you.

GUIDED PRAYER

1. Meditate on the availability of knowing the living God. Allow Scripture to stir up your desire to seek him with all your heart.

"Be still, and know that I am God. I will be exalted among the nations, I will be exalted in the earth!" Psalm 46:10

"You have said, 'Seek my face.' My heart says to you, 'Your face, Lord, do I seek.'" Psalm 27:8

"But this is the covenant that I will make with the house of Israel after those days, declares the Lord: I will put my law within them, and I will write it on their hearts. And I will be their God, and they shall be my people. And no longer shall each one teach his neighbor and each his brother, saying, 'Know the Lord,' for they shall all know me, from the least of them to the greatest, declares the Lord. For I will forgive their iniquity, and I will remember their sin no more." Jeremiah 31:33-34

2. Is your life centered around the pursuit of knowing God? Check the posture of your heart today. Look at the way you spend your time, your emotions, your thoughts, and your actions. What seems to be your greatest pursuit?

3. Spend some time centering your heart around true relationship with a knowable God. Ask him to help guide your heart through your day toward this pursuit. Ask him to give you a check in your heart when something takes his place as the greatest desire in your life. Live today with him as your highest priority.

"With my whole heart I seek you; let me not wander from your commandments!" Psalm 119:10

Jeremiah 9:23-24 says,

Let not the wise man boast in his wisdom, let not the mighty man boast in his might, let not the rich man boast in his riches, but let him who boasts boast in this, that he understands and knows me, that I am the Lord who practices steadfast love, justice, and righteousness in the earth. For in these things I delight, declares the Lord.

May we be those who boast solely in our relationship with God. May his love and nearness be our highest joy. And may it be said of us at the end of our days that we sought the Lord above all else.

Extended Reading: Psalm 46

The Experience of His Love

DAY 16

DEVOTIONAL

There is nothing in this world like experiencing the unconditional love of God. His love extends farther than the width of the skies. His love goes deeper than the deepest sea. His love is more powerful than a raging fire, and it is closer than the heartbeat within your chest. Experiencing his love is like becoming new again and again. With each taste of his affection, the wounds of the past become healed and restored that one no longer regrets pain but rejoices in the opportunity it gives to experience the love of a good and near heavenly Father once again.

"And hope does not put us to shame, because God's love has been poured into our hearts through the Holy Spirit who has been given to us."

ROMANS 5:5

When we seek to know God we gain experiences with his love because it's who he is. 1 John 4:8 says, *"Anyone who does not love does not know God, because God is love."* To know love is to know God because every bit of true love comes from him. 1 John 4:16 says, *"So we have come to know and to believe the love that God has for us. God is love, and whoever abides in love abides in God, and God abides in him."* It's time for you and me to *"believe the love that God has for us."* It's time that we cease questioning whether we are loved and instead seek the face of our heavenly Father that we might know beyond a shadow of a doubt that he loves us.

Almost all of my energy goes toward being loved. I look for love everywhere. I look for it from my wife, friends, coworkers, acquaintances, and total strangers. I constantly concern myself with whether I am, moment by moment, loved or not. But Jesus came that we might no longer ask ourselves that question.

"For God so loved the world, that he gave his only Son, that whoever believes in him should not perish but have eternal life" (John 3:16). God already loved us so much that he died for us (Romans 5:8). There's nothing we have to do to earn his love. If we need a fresh reminder of it, all we have to do is simply seek his face and love will come as the result.

We have unlimited access by the grace of God to the love of God. Unconditional, limitless love awaits us at every turn if our hearts will simply seek his. Scripture says in Psalm 27:8, *"You have said, 'Seek my face.' My heart says to you, 'Your face, Lord, do I seek.'"* May we be children who constantly seek the face of our loving heavenly Father. May we be a bride wholly wrapped up in the love of our Bridegroom. And may we experience as the result of simply seeking God the powerful affections of a God who laid down his own life for the sake of his creation.

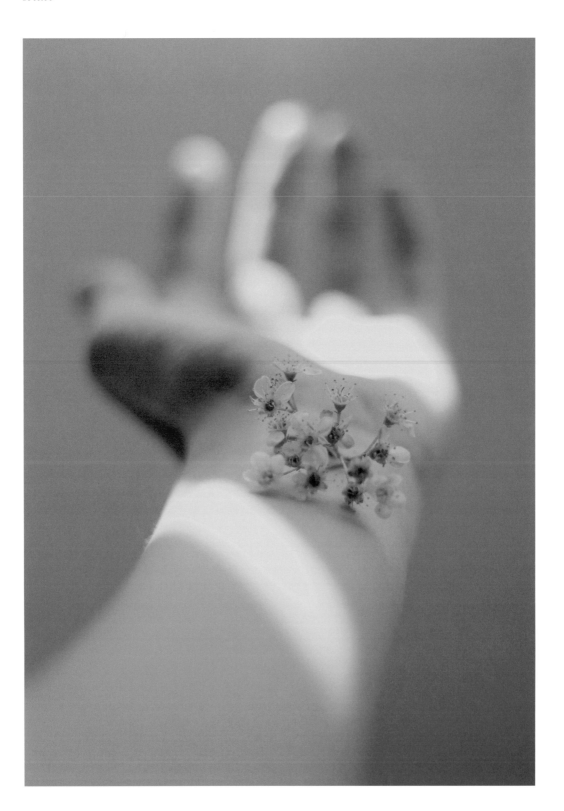

GUIDED PRAYER

1. Meditate on the love of your heavenly Father. Allow Scripture to stir up your desire to seek God and as a result experience an encounter with his love.

"Anyone who does not love does not know God, because God is love." 1 John 4:8

"For God so loved the world, that he gave his only Son, that whoever believes in him should not perish but have eternal life." John 3:16

"So we have come to know and to believe the love that God has for us. God is love, and whoever abides in love abides in God, and God abides in him." 1 John 4:16

2. Where are you seeking love? To whom or what are you turning for love other than God?

3. Take time to seek the face of your heavenly Father and encounter his love. Open your heart to him and simply desire relationship with him. He will take care of the rest.

"And hope does not put us to shame, because God's love has been poured into our hearts through the Holy Spirit who has been given to us." Romans 5:5

"You have said, 'Seek my face.' My heart says to you, 'Your face, Lord, do I seek.'" Psalm 27:8

1 John 4:18 says, *"There is no fear in love, but perfect love casts out fear. For fear has to do with punishment, and whoever fears has not been perfected in love."* We have no reason to fear seeking God. All that he would say to us, do in us, and lead us to comes from a foundation of his perfect love. There is no reason to fear in this life. There is nothing here that can separate us from eternal, unbound relationship with our heavenly Father. Allow his love to cast out any reservations you have today. Receive an awareness of his perfect love and rest easy in his kindness.

Extended Reading: 1 John 4

The Experience of His Voice

DEVOTIONAL

To seek the fullness of relationship with God is to hear his voice. *"Whoever is of God hears the words of God"* (John 8:47). Just like when I seek true relationship with a person, a conversation must happen; when we seek to truly know God, he talks with us. He is not a God who is silent but a God who speaks to us in any and every way he can.

All throughout the New Testament, there is both teaching on hearing the voice of God and instances where the people of God had conversation with him. In John 14:16-17 Jesus says, *"And I will ask the Father, and he will give you another Helper, to be with you forever, even the Spirit of truth, whom the world cannot receive, because it neither sees him nor knows him. You know him, for he dwells with you and will be in you."* And later in John 16:13 Jesus says, *"When the Spirit of truth comes, he will guide you into all the truth, for he will not speak on his own authority, but whatever he hears he will speak, and he will declare to you the things that are to come."*

God himself dwells within us and longs to speak to our hearts. He longs for us to know the will of our heavenly Father the way Jesus did. He longs for us to follow his leading moment by moment the way

*"Whoever is of God hears
the words of God."*

JOHN 8:47

the apostles did. And he longs for us to engage in conversation with him as all those who are in true relationship with one another do.

God is constantly speaking to us. The problem is that we don't know how to listen. Scripture tells us that he is declaring the invisible attributes of his nature through creation (Romans 1:20). When I take time to experience firsthand the things God has made, I feel his presence. There is a reason it's peaceful to be in creation. There is a reason it's restful to be in the mountains, lay on a beach, or swim in the sea. All of creation is declaring the wonderful character of our loving God. We just need to learn how to listen.

God speaks to us through his revealed word. The inspirer of Scripture dwells within us and longs to use the Bible as a wonderful avenue to encountering its Author. The Bible is not a biography written after someone has died. Rather, it is the living, active words of a living, active God who longs for relationship with us (Hebrews 4:12).

God speaks to us through one another. All of us as believers have been given the same Spirit who has called us to a lifestyle of encouraging one another.

We are called to be a critical part of the process of discovering God's heart and will in each other's lives. If we will make time to learn how God speaks to us for others, we will discover the very words of God given by grace to the lips of man.

And God speaks to us directly from his Spirit to our spirit. The Holy Spirit is a vocal God. He longs for us to know his thoughts. He longs to direct us whether it be through words, a sense, a desire, an uneasiness, or a prompting. He is always speaking to us. In order to learn to hear his voice moment by moment, whether we're in solitude or in chaos, we must make time in the secret place to seek the fullness of relationship with him. It's in seeking relationship with God that we become familiar with his voice and are able to follow him as sheep with their Shepherd.

Take time in guided prayer to seek the face of your heavenly Father and hear his voice however he is choosing to speak. Don't limit yourself to hearing him in only one way. The path to the fullness of relationship with him is marked by his voice in each of these ways and more. Open your heart to hearing him through any and every way he is speaking that you might grow in your relationship with a good and loving God.

89

GUIDED PRAYER

1. Meditate on Scripture that declares God to be a vocal God. Allow Scripture to stir up your desire to hear God in every way he speaks.

"My sheep hear my voice, and I know them, and they follow me." John 10:27

"Whoever is of God hears the words of God." John 8:47

"Behold, I stand at the door and knock. If anyone hears my voice and opens the door, I will come in to him and eat with him, and he with me." Revelation 3:20

2. In what ways are you comfortable hearing God? What ways might be new to you? Know that there is grace to grow in every facet of your relationship with him. Don't limit yourself to only what you've known or experienced up to this point. Rather, seek the truth of God's word by his Spirit and discover a wealth of relationship you might not have yet experienced.

3. Choose one of the ways God speaks that's new to you and ask him to help you have conversation with him through that avenue. Again, hearing his voice through all of these avenues is meant to be the byproduct of simply seeking relationship with him. Just as we don't seek to hear the voice of another person but seek relationship with them and get a conversation as a result, simply seek to know God and talk with him.

"Call to me and I will answer you, and will tell you great and hidden things that you have not known." Jeremiah 33:3

"And your ears shall hear a word behind you, saying, 'This is the way, walk in it,' when you turn to the right or when you turn to the left." Isaiah 30:21

"When the Spirit of truth comes, he will guide you into all the truth, for he will not speak on his own authority, but whatever he hears he will speak, and he will declare to you the things that are to come." John 16:13

To have conversation with God might sound strange for some, but that doesn't mean it doesn't happen. Rather, to have conversation with God available to us and to not take advantage of it is strange. God longs to speak to you. The Creator of all longs to have dialogue with you. The King of kings and Lord of lords is inviting you to meet with him that you might have true relationship. Seek God with all your heart. Look to Scripture and the lives of biblical believers as your source of truth and normalcy. Because of God's heart to speak to you, you can live your life in constant conversation with a God who is both near to you and loves you.

Extended Reading: John 10

The Experience
of His Peace

DAY 18

DEVOTIONAL

One of the most heavenly aspects of experiencing God is his abounding peace. Peace is not something this world can offer us. This world is run on chaos, stress, confusion, striving, and frivolous pursuits with no satisfaction. Even in this life, God offers us the peace of heaven, the peace that comes from having our hearts wrapped up in true relationship with him.

Philippians 4:6-7 says, *"Do not be anxious about anything, but in everything by prayer and supplication with thanksgiving let your requests be made known to God. And the peace of God, which surpasses all understanding, will guard your hearts and your*

"Now may the Lord of peace himself give you peace at all times in every way. The Lord be with you all."

2 THESSALONIANS 3:16

minds in Christ Jesus." God exchanges our earthly cares and stresses for his heavenly, sustaining peace. He is such a good Father to us that he takes that which troubles our hearts, promises to take care of us down to the smallest burden, and offers us incomprehensible peace from his Spirit.

Jesus says in John 16:33, *"I have said these things to you, that in me you may have peace. In the world you will have tribulation. But take heart; I have overcome the world."* When we seek relationship with Jesus we are seeking relationship with the One who conquered death and destroyed any and every scheme of the enemy against us. To know him is to know a true Conqueror. And in knowing him our lives become wrapped up in his. Our worried and fearful hearts become wrapped up in his heart of peace.

Isaiah 26:3 says, *"You keep him in perfect peace whose mind is stayed on you, because he trusts in you."* God longs for us to so encounter his trustworthiness that our lives are marked by his peace. He longs for us to so trust him that this world cannot rob us of the peace that comes from knowing our God will always prove himself faithful. All he has promised to do he will do. All he has said of himself he truly is. Peace comes from keeping our mind stayed on the perfect character of our heavenly Father and letting who he is be at the foundation of all we do, think, and feel.

God has heavenly peace in store for you today. The peace he offers you isn't of this world and therefore will sustain you through any of its troubles (John 14:27). Come before your loving heavenly Father and cast your cares on him. Let your requests be made known to him. Place your trust in his trustworthiness. And receive the perfect, sustaining peace of your loving Father.

May your day today be marked by the fruit of wholehearted relationship with the God of peace.

GUIDED PRAYER

1. Meditate on the peace available to you in relationship with God. Allow Scripture to help you not settle for stress, burdens, and cares that aren't your portion in Jesus.

"Peace I leave with you; my peace I give to you. Not as the world gives do I give to you. Let not your hearts be troubled, neither let them be afraid." John 14:27

"I have said these things to you, that in me you may have peace. In the world you will have tribulation. But take heart; I have overcome the world." John 16:33

"You keep him in perfect peace whose mind is stayed on you, because he trusts in you." Isaiah 26:3

"For God is not a God of confusion but of peace." 1 Corinthians 14:33

2. What has been causing you stress? What's been stealing your peace? What thoughts, people, situations, fears, or spiritual attacks do you need to bring before your loving heavenly Father?

3. *"Cast all your anxieties on him, because he cares for you"* (1 Peter 5:6-7). Take time to bring before God all that's bothering you. Lay all your anxieties at his feet, choose to trust that he will take care of them and help you through them, and receive his peace that surpasses all understanding.

"Do not be anxious about anything, but in everything by prayer and supplication with thanksgiving let your requests be made known to God. And the peace of God, which surpasses all understanding, will guard your hearts and your minds in Christ Jesus." Philippians 4:6-7

"Now may the Lord of peace himself give you peace at all times in every way. The Lord be with you all." 2 Thessalonians 3:16

"But the fruit of the Spirit is love, joy, peace, patience, kindness, goodness, faithfulness, gentleness, self-control; against such things there is no law." Galatians 5:22-23

Romans 8:6 says, *"For to set the mind on the flesh is death, but to set the mind on the Spirit is life and peace."* We have the choice moment by moment to set our minds on the things of this world or on the things of God. When we choose to set our minds on the Spirit, we are positioning ourselves to be people marked by the fruit of his presence in our lives. When we choose the world we are only setting ourselves up for failure, anxiety, and trouble. Choose today to set your mind on the Lord in every situation. The things of this world are fleeting, but our God spans throughout the farthest reaches of eternity. May his power, faithfulness, and nearness bring you peace today.

Extended Reading: Philippians 4

Partnering in His Purposes

DAY 19

DEVOTIONAL

True friends are those who are willing to partner with us in things that really matter to us. True friends are willing to help simply because they love us, even if the task isn't something they would have ordinarily valued. In John 21:15 we gain insight into a conversation between two friends, Jesus and Simon Peter. Scripture says,

When they had finished breakfast, Jesus said to Simon Peter, "Simon, son of John, do you love me more than these?" He said to him, "Yes, Lord; you know that I love you." He said to him, "Feed my lambs."

"But you are a chosen race, a royal priesthood, a holy nation, a people for his own possession, that you may proclaim the excellencies of him who called you out of darkness into his marvelous light."

1 PETER 2:9

Jesus didn't ask Simon Peter if his heart burned for taking care of his people. He didn't ask Peter his plans after Jesus had gone. After being established in the heart of Peter as Lord, Jesus simply asked him if he loved him.

I've spent so much of my life trying to figure out what I liked—what I felt like doing. I've taken all the gift tests, personality tests, and strength tests. And while God absolutely fashions, forms, and equips us for unique purposes, I believe God is asking the same question of you and me that he did of Peter. I believe that our purposes are to be foundationally birthed out of utter devotion to Jesus above what we want or feel equipped to do.

Jesus is looking for disciples who will say yes to that which is greater than they could have ever imagined doing. He's looking for friends like Simon Peter who will follow him wherever he leads, even if it means to their death. He's looking for those who are so in love with him that at a single statement from his lips we willingly and obediently respond by taking up our cross as he did and living a surrendered, purposeful life.

Take time today to hear the voice of your Lord saying, *"Do you love me?"* Assess today whether he truly is your greatest love. And in response, open your heart to receive any command he would speak to you today. If you are faithful to respond with your life, you will find his strength to accomplish any purpose and the reality of his love to be your unshakable joy.

GUIDED PRAYER

1. Meditate on John 21:15. Allow the word of God to search your heart.

"When they had finished breakfast, Jesus said to Simon Peter, 'Simon, son of John, do you love me more than these?' He said to him, 'Yes, Lord; you know that I love you.' He said to him, 'Feed my lambs.'" John 21:15

2. Assess whether Jesus truly is your greatest love. If he isn't—if you wouldn't follow him anywhere—take time to surrender anything you've placed above him. Confess any idols you have in your life that he might truly be crowned King of your heart today.

"Those who pay regard to vain idols forsake their hope of steadfast love." Jonah 2:8

3. Ask him to speak his will to you today. Ask him what he would have you do and where he would have you do it. Be faithful to respond in obedience and trust today.

"Whoever has my commandments and keeps them, he it is who loves me. And he who loves me will be loved by my Father, and I will love him and manifest myself to him." John 14:21

"But you are a chosen race, a royal priesthood, a holy nation, a people for his own possession, that you may proclaim the excellencies of him who called you out of darkness into his marvelous light." 1 Peter 2:9

In John 15:12-14 Jesus said, *"This is my commandment, that you love one another as I have loved you. Greater love has no one than this, that someone lay down his life for his friends. You are my friends if you do what I command you."* Rather than placing yourself at the center of your thoughts, actions, motives, and emotions, choose to center your life around others today. Choose to serve and love others as Jesus did. Ask the Holy Spirit to give you his heart for those around you that you might be a reflection of his great love in the earth. Seeing God's kingdom come is nothing more than choosing to love and live as Jesus did. You can be a conduit for his purposes in the earth today. May your day be filled with spectacular wonders as God manifests his kingdom through your life.

Extended Reading: John 12

The Experience of His Freedom

SCRIPTURE

"What shall we say then? Are we to continue in sin that grace may abound? By no means! How can we who died to sin still live in it? Do you not know that all of us who have been baptized into Christ Jesus were baptized into his death? We were buried therefore with him by baptism into death, in order that, just as Christ was raised from the dead by the glory of the Father, we too might walk in newness of life." Romans 6:1-4

DEVOTIONAL

The Christian experience of freedom was not established by the power and endurance of mankind, but by the sacrifice and love of our God. The freedom we experience is not our own, but his. Apart from the redemption bought for us, we have no strength to resist sin. And apart from continually renewing our minds to the truth of this redemption, we'll continue to act as if chains that were broken long ago still tie us down to the world from which we've been successfully ransomed. Paul says in Romans 6:1-4,

What shall we say then? Are we to continue in sin that grace may abound? By no means! How can we who died to sin still live in it? Do you not know that all of us who have been baptized into Christ Jesus were baptized into his death? We were buried therefore with him by baptism into death, in order that, just as Christ was raised from the dead by the glory of the Father, we too might walk in newness of life.

To experience freedom here on earth is to continuously acknowledge that our old ways—our former self—was buried with Christ the day we accepted him as Lord. To sin is to live outside of the reality that we've been given a new resurrected identity in Christ, our resurrected King.

How do you see yourself in regard to your sin today? How do you believe you experience freedom? In what areas of your life are you still trying in your own strength to fight for something Jesus already bought with his blood? What sin have you not yet brought to the glorious light of God's powerful resurrection that you might see it for what it truly is?

There is freedom for you today in Christ that's available apart from any past failures, present downfalls, or future concerns. You can *"walk in newness of life"* as you live in the reality of the inner working of the Holy Spirit and follow his leadership away from your old identity. Your mistakes don't change the reality of God's grace. Your sin is powerless to bind you. Your freedom is just as sure as the limitless love of your Savior.

Take time today to renew your mind to who you are in Christ. Take time to bring your sin to the light and confess it that God might take it from you as far as the east is from the west. May you experience the freedom of your risen King today as you live in light of his powerful grace.

GUIDED PRAYER

1. Meditate on what the Bible says about freedom from sin. Align your understanding of your sin with the truth of God's word.

"But now that you have been set free from sin and have become slaves of God, the fruit you get leads to sanctification and its end, eternal life." Romans 6:22

"Do you not know that all of us who have been baptized into Christ Jesus were baptized into his death? We were buried therefore with him by baptism into death, in order that, just as Christ was raised from the dead by the glory of the Father, we too might walk in newness of life." Romans 6:3-4

"And by him everyone who believes is freed from everything from which you could not be freed by the law of Moses." Acts 13:39

2. What sin do you need to bring to God today in confession? What feels too dark and too powerful to gain freedom from? Bring it to him that you might see it in light of his power and sacrifice.

3. Ask God to reveal how he sees you. Ask him to reveal your new identity in him. Ask him how you can experience freedom from that which doesn't align with your new identity.

Renewing our minds to our new identity takes time. Often, while we are gaining a correct understanding of our freedom, we need to set up boundaries to gain separation from darkness. Take time to identify things that continuously lead you into temptation. It could be friends, media, or actions that seem beneficial, like lifting weights or going shopping. Ask the Holy Spirit to help you establish boundaries that will guard your heart from the outside as he does a powerful work in you on the inside. May you experience the freedom purchased for you by the blood of Jesus as you *"walk in newness of life"* with the power of the Holy Spirit.

Extended Reading: Romans 6

The Experience of His Presence

DAY 21

DEVOTIONAL

Experiencing the presence of God sounds like such a mystery. It sounds like this wonderful but evasive thing that some people get sometimes, but isn't concrete enough to expect or place your hope in. We associate God's presence with emotions and music as if it were a breeze so light and momentary you almost couldn't be sure it happened at all.

"One thing have I asked of the Lord, that will I seek after: that I may dwell in the house of the Lord all the days of my life, to gaze upon the beauty of the Lord and to inquire in his temple."

PSALM 27:4

But in reality God's presence is as simple as being in the presence of a friend or spouse. It's as simple and concrete as being around a person except for one simple truth: God never leaves. And just as you can be in the same room as a friend and not know it, you can live the Christian life apart from experiencing God's nearness. Just as you can be sitting right across from a friend and be so busy with technology or your own thoughts to even remember they are there, you can go through life focused on the busyness of present circumstances and miss out on the fact that God is closer than your breath.

But we find hope for encountering the presence of God in Psalm 27:4. Scripture says, *"One thing have I asked of the Lord, that will I seek after: that I may dwell in the house of the Lord all the days of my life, to gaze upon the beauty of the Lord and to inquire in his temple."* This pursuit, this action of seeking the living God, never comes back empty. To seek God is to encounter God. Emotions aside, complexities cast away—God is already with you. He is already closer than he could ever be. His Spirit, his presence

in the earth, never leaves you and never forsakes you. And when you turn your attention toward him, just as you can to a friend sitting across a table from you, you can encounter him.

Psalm 139:7 says, *"Where shall I go from your Spirit? Or where shall I flee from your presence?"* His presence is always available. He's not a friend who turns away from you or hides his heart. He's not a small gust of wind that comes and goes as he pleases. He's a God who would suffer and die that he might tear the veil and make his presence fully, continuously available to all those who would seek him. He's a God who's working tirelessly to restore his crown of creation to himself that we might walk with him like in the Garden of Eden, but this time for all of eternity with no possibility of a fall or barrier between us.

Your ability to meet with God is as simple as turning your attention toward him and allowing yourself to be known. May you meet with your heavenly Father in profoundly simple ways today as you enter into a time of guided prayer.

GUIDED PRAYER

1. Meditate on the availability of God's presence.

"Where shall I go from your Spirit? Or where shall I flee from your presence?" Psalm 139:7

"You will seek me and find me, when you seek me with all your heart." Jeremiah 29:13

2. What's your greatest fear regarding God's presence. What's something that would keep you from seeking after him like you would a close friend?

"There is no fear in love, but perfect love casts out fear." 1 John 4:18

3. Surrender any hesitation you have to him and seek him in faith that he is already with you. Turn your heart toward him and talk to him honestly and openly. Allow him to reveal his nearness to you in any way he wishes.

"One thing have I asked of the Lord, that will I seek after: that I may dwell in the house of the Lord all the days of my life, to gaze upon the beauty of the Lord and to inquire in his temple." Psalm 27:4

The best place to start with God is always honesty. He doesn't meet you in a place that isn't real. So if you're trying to seek him but avoiding something, you are attempting to sew back together the veil he so lovingly tore in two. There's no need to veil your heart from him. There's no reason to act as if everything is all right if it isn't. Whether you're at church, with friends, or meeting him in the secret place, he only asks for honesty from you. Tell him how you feel. Open up the places of your heart that you are too shameful or scared to let into the light. Allow him to flood your fears with his relentless love and experience the presence that only grace has to offer.

Extended Reading: Psalm 27

God speaks

04

WEEK

*"Incline your ear, and come
to me; hear, that your soul
may live." Isaiah 55:3*

WEEKLY OVERVIEW

You and I have been given the invaluable gift of communication with God. Just as we have been learning the past few weeks, God's presence is always available, and speaking with him is as simple as speaking with a close friend. This week we will explore the various ways God chooses to reveal himself to us. May your communion with God flourish as you engage in continual conversation with your loving, present heavenly Father.

God Speaks

DAY 22

DEVOTIONAL

For too much of my Christian life I believed God didn't like to talk. My experience led me to think that God only spoke a few times in history and only to people like Moses, David or Paul, but never to a person like me. Then one day God spoke to me. I asked him a question out of desperation and he spoke. The Creator of the universe broke through the walls of my misconceptions and spoke to my heart in a voice so clear it couldn't be mistaken.

"Call to me and I will answer you,
and will tell you great and hidden
things that you have not known."

JEREMIAH 33:3

After God spoke to me so clearly, I began to take time to listen. And in making space for God to speak, my life began to be transformed by consistent, internal conversation with my heavenly Father. You see, Scripture makes it clear that God loves to talk with his children. John 8:47 says, *"Whoever is of God hears the words of God."* Jeremiah 33:3 says, *"Call to me and I will answer you, and will tell you great and hidden things that you have not known."* Isaiah 55:3 says, *"Incline your ear, and come to me; hear, that your soul may live."* Psalm 32:8 says, *"I will instruct you and teach you in the way you should go; I will counsel you with my eye upon you."* The list of Scriptures goes on and on. In story after story the people of God hear God and know his will. The Bible is clear that God speaks to all of us as his children in a way we can understand through any and every means possible.

God speaks through all sorts of avenues. Most assuredly, he speaks to us through his Word. The Bible is one of our greatest gifts as Christians. It is the very word of God, *"living and active, sharper than any two-edged sword, piercing to the division of soul and of spirit, of joints and of marrow, and discerning the thoughts and intentions of the heart"* (Hebrews 4:12). God also speaks directly to us through his Holy Spirit. John 16:13 says, *"When the Spirit of truth comes, he will guide you into all the truth, for he will not speak on*

his own authority, but whatever he hears he will speak, and he will declare to you the things that are to come." And Scripture reveals how God speaks through his creation. Romans 1:20 says that God's *"invisible attributes, namely, his eternal power and divine nature, have been clearly perceived, ever since the creation of the world, in the things that have been made."*

God loves to speak. He isn't silent. He isn't distant. He longs for you to live with the knowledge of his love and perfect will. The question isn't whether God speaks. The question is, will you listen? Will you choose to submit yourself to him—to receive and obey what he would tell you? The first time God spoke directly to me he asked me to do something incredibly difficult. It didn't make total sense. But I knew he spoke. And in submission I obeyed his command and my life has been different ever since.

Listen to God today. Quiet your soul and receive the gift of conversation with your heavenly Father. God has placed his Spirit within you—closer to you than you can fully comprehend. You are unified with God. Ask the Spirit to reveal to you God's word today. Ask God to make you aware of any and every avenue he desires to speak through. Then listen with an obedient, receptive heart to all the wonderful things he longs to tell you.

GUIDED PRAYER

1. Take time to quiet your soul. Confess anything that you feel is in the way of your relationship with God. Hand over to him anything that's troubling your mind. Receive his peace, and wait patiently for him to speak.

"Incline your ear, and come to me; hear, that your soul may live." Isaiah 55:3

2. Listen. Ask the Spirit how God feels about you. Ask him for his will and direction. Pay attention to any thoughts, inclinations or changes in your emotions that come from the Holy Spirit. Allow God to speak in any way he wants.

"Call to me and I will answer you, and will tell you great and hidden things that you have not known." Jeremiah 33:3

3. Now thank God for speaking. Worship him because he isn't distant. Let the truth of his nearness transform your perspective and emotions today.

Listen to God throughout your day. Engage with him in consistent conversation. Practice listening to him in all circumstances. Ask for his help and understanding in anything that troubles you. The rest of this week we'll be practicing hearing God through different ways he chooses to speak. May this week lead you into a deeper and more satisfying relationship with your heavenly Father as you engage with him in continual conversation.

Extended Reading: John 8

God Speaks through His Word

DEVOTIONAL

Deuteronomy 8:3 teaches us that, *"Man does not live by bread alone, but man lives by every word that comes from the mouth of the Lord."* The word of the Lord when planted in good soil produces abundant, life-giving fruit (Matthew 13:20-22). We have in Scripture a feast that satisfies the deepest places of our hearts no food or drink could ever satiate.

"Man does not live by bread alone, but man lives by every word that comes from the mouth of the Lord."

DEUTERONOMY 8:3

When you open your Bible, you are literally opening the words of God. Scripture is God's voice available for you in every moment, situation, and predicament you face. You can know God desires to speak to you because you have in your possession his voice through the Bible. God desires to reveal to you his will because he has given you his Spirit to *"guide you into all the truth, for he will not speak on his own authority, but whatever he hears he will speak, and he will declare to you the things that are to come"* (John 16:13).

When you read Scripture with the help of your teacher, the Holy Spirit, the Bible is no longer just a book written thousands of years ago but a source of life-giving revelation. Read the Bible prayerfully, paying attention to any words, phrases, or ideas that stand out to you.

Allow God to apply Scripture directly to your life through his Spirit. And as you read, submit yourself to God's word with a continual "yes" in your heart. Choose to be a doer of the word that you might be blessed in everything you do (James 1:22-25).

God's word is only as impactful as you are willing to be obedient. The power of Scripture becomes evident as you daily submit yourself to it. So today as you read God's word, ask the Spirit to highlight phrases and ideas, submit yourself in obedience to what Scripture says, and be a doer of the word. God is ready to speak to you. He is prepared to sow the seed of his voice wherever it's welcome. Open your heart to the word of God, and allow it to produce the fruit of joy, peace, and purpose in your life.

GUIDED PRAYER

1. Ask the Spirit what you should read today. Pay attention to anything you feel like reading or pick from John 17 or Proverbs 3. Meditate on any phrases, words, or ideas that stand out to you.

"Man does not live by bread alone, but man lives by every word that comes from the mouth of the Lord." Deuteronomy 8:3

2. Submit yourself to the word of God. Allow Scripture to be the foundation for all your thoughts, emotions, and perspectives. Allow God's word to influence and transform any parts of your life that don't align with it.

3. Now commit yourself to follow through with any action that God's word requires. Ask God what he would have you do with what he's shown you. Choose to be a doer of the word.

"Be doers of the word, and not hearers only, deceiving yourselves. For if anyone is a hearer of the word and not a doer, he is like a man who looks intently at his natural face in a mirror. For he looks at himself and goes away and at once forgets what he was like. But the one who looks into the perfect law, the law of liberty, and perseveres, being no hearer who forgets but a doer who acts, he will be blessed in his doing." James 1:22-25

If you aren't in the habit of reading God's word daily, look for a Bible reading plan or book of the Bible you can read consistently. We were made to feast on the life-giving words of Scripture. God's word can't produce abundant fruit in your life if you aren't consuming it. May your day be transformed as you seek to live in faithful obedience to the word of God.

Extended Reading: Proverbs 3

Hearing God's Voice

DAY 24

DEVOTIONAL

God desires to speak directly to you. As a good Father, he longs to engage with you in continual conversation. So great was his longing for communication that he's given you the gift of the Holy Spirit. You now have access to the heart of God through the Spirit. You can know his will, hear his voice, and live with the knowledge of his love.

"When the Spirit of truth comes, he will guide you into all the truth, for he will not speak on his own authority, but whatever he hears he will speak, and he will declare to you the things that are to come."

JOHN 16:13

John 16:13 says, *"When the Spirit of truth comes, he will guide you into all the truth, for he will not speak on his own authority, but whatever he hears he will speak, and he will declare to you the things that are to come."* If you are a Christian, the *"Spirit of truth"* has come. He dwells within you. He longs to tell you how God feels about you. He longs to guide you to the Father's perfect, hopeful, and pleasing plans (Jeremiah 29:11). His voice is perfect, full of love, and always truthful. He will never guide you into something that isn't best for you. He will never speak hate or condemnation to you. As John 16:13 promises, he will declare to you what he hears the Father say.

Let the truth that God desires to have real, life-transforming conversations with you sink into your heart for a minute. Think about what it means for your own life to have communication with God. Your Creator longs to help you with your decisions, relationships, work, finances, and identity. God himself wants to talk with you about your life—to fully know you and be known by you.

Just as any good parent loves talking with their children, your heavenly Father loves talking to you, his child. You see, God speaking to you is so little about your ability to hear his voice and so much more about his desire for you to know him. His voice in your life is just another product of grace, God's unmerited favor for those who believe. Like any conversation, you will only hear him when you are listening. And just like any good conversation, God longs to hear from you as well.

Hebrews 11:6 says, *"And without faith it is impossible to please him, for whoever would draw near to God must believe that he exists and that he rewards those who seek him."* Have faith that God longs to speak to you. Draw near to him in the assurance that he is already filled with love for you. The Holy Spirit longs to have a communicative relationship with you. Let the weight of conversation with God rest on his shoulders, trust in his word and his character, and listen to whatever he would speak to you today.

As you enter into guided prayer, take time to quiet your heart and listen to the voice of the Spirit.

GUIDED PRAYER

1. Take a moment to quiet your mind and soul. Receive God's presence and meditate on the important truth that the Spirit speaks.

"When the Spirit of truth comes, he will guide you into all the truth, for he will not speak on his own authority, but whatever he hears he will speak, and he will declare to you the things that are to come." John 16:13

2. Now listen to God. If you have a situation, question or anything you want to ask him, now is the time! God longs for you to tell him what you want help with. If you just want to know how he feels about you, ask him! Again, the weight of God speaking is on him. Trust him and his timing. God does desire to speak to you.

3. Write down whatever God tells you. Rest in the goodness of what he's spoken.

Communicating with God is similar to engaging in conversation with a close friend. I don't go to my friend and ask them to tell me anything so I know they are real. Rather, I seek to know them as a person and conversation takes place as a result. Seek to know God as deeply as possible. Trust that he is real and that he speaks. Talk with him because you simply want to know him. And rest in the fact that you will have conversation with your loving heavenly Father throughout eternity. May your day be marked by life-giving conversation with the Holy Spirit.

Extended Reading: Psalm 27

God Speaks through His Creation

DEVOTIONAL

Nature has an ability to bring me peace in a way nothing else does. Sure I get annoyed by bugs or tired from hiking. But seeing the beauty, creativity, and complexity of what God has made has had a profound effect on my spiritual life. Have you ever just spent some time in God's creation? Maybe it was hiking, lying on the beach, swimming in an ocean or a lake, fishing, gazing over the grand canyon, driving through the mountains, watching a thunderstorm or just playing in the rain. Take a minute to reflect on that time and what you felt. Looking back,

do think you might have felt God's presence? Did the awe and wonder of nature's splendor bring you peace, or even lead you to thoughts about God?

The more I've come to know God the more there has grown in me an adoration and appreciation for his creation. Romans 1:20 states that God's *"invisible attributes, namely, his eternal power and divine nature, have been clearly perceived, ever since the creation of the world, in the things that have been made."* Nature is meant

"For his invisible attributes, namely, his eternal power and divine nature, have been clearly perceived, ever since the creation of the world, in the things that have been made."

ROMANS 1:20

to declare to us the *"invisible attributes"* of God. And Scripture is clear that God is at work in his creation—maintaining and facilitating all that happens in the world. Psalm 147:8-9, 15-18 tells us,

He covers the heavens with clouds; he prepares rain for the earth; he makes grass grow on the hills. He gives to the beasts their food, and to the young ravens that cry... He sends out his command to the earth; his word runs swiftly. He gives snow like wool; he scatters frost like ashes. He hurls down his crystals of ice like crumbs; who can stand before his cold? He sends out his word, and melts them; he makes his wind blow and the waters flow.

When you see animals eating, you are witnessing God's provision in the earth and can, as a result, know that he will provide for you. When you see snow fall, ice form, and springtime come to melt away the cold you can know that God is at work around you and in your life. To miss out on all creation speaks to us is to miss an important part of God's voice.

You see, while God does an incredible job taking care of a world wrought with the effects of sin, he promises to take care of you even more. Jesus commands us in Matthew 6:26-30,

Look at the birds of the air: they neither sow nor reap nor gather into barns, and yet your heavenly Father feeds them. Are you not of more value than they? And

which of you by being anxious can add a single hour to his span of life? And why are you anxious about clothing? Consider the lilies of the field, how they grow: they neither toil nor spin, yet I tell you, even Solomon in all his glory was not arrayed like one of these. But if God so clothes the grass of the field, which today is alive and tomorrow is thrown into the oven, will he not much more clothe you, O you of little faith?

Jesus teaches us to look upon creation and listen as it declares to us the nature of God. In fact, he commands us to do so. You can look at the grass of the field and know of God's unwavering faithfulness for you. You can look at the birds and never wonder if you will get your next meal. Nature declares to us that God has and will provide for us all of our days. Nature tells us not to worry because God is both powerful and near. Nature tells us that God is creative, practical, brilliant, loving, and full of mystery and wonder. Nature tells us that God speaks.

God created the cosmos so that you might have another mysterious yet clear way of hearing his voice. Whether you live in the city or country, look upon God's creation and listen for his voice. Ask him what he wants you to know as you see all the wonders of his hands. Let the beauty and mystery of all of God's creation fill you with a deeper longing to know your heavenly Father. Listen to God today and allow your heart to be stirred as you discover his unwavering desire to speak to you through his creation.

GUIDED PRAYER

1. Take some time to go out in God's creation.

2. Now ask God what he wants to tell you through his creation. Let him speak in whatever way he desires.

"For his invisible attributes, namely, his eternal power and divine nature, have been clearly perceived, ever since the creation of the world, in the things that have been made."
Romans 1:20

3. Meditate on the truth he reveals to your heart and take some time to rest in his presence.

As children of an infinite, paradoxical God we must learn to embrace and value mystery. God longs to speak through his creation. He longs to satisfy your longing for fascination as you ponder the mystery and beauty of that which we will never fully understand. May you hear the loving voice of the Father today as you allow the Creator to speak through his creation.

Extended Reading: Psalm 19

God Speaks
through Meditation

DAY 26

DEVOTIONAL

The spiritual discipline of meditation does for the heart of a Christian what nutrients and good soil do for the seed of a plant. Through meditation the seed of God's word takes root and produces life-giving, abundant fruit. Richard Foster in his book *Celebration of Discipline* wrote, "The purpose of

*"I will meditate on your precepts
and fix my eyes on your ways."*

PSALM 119:15

meditation is to enable us to hear God more clearly. Meditation is listening, sensing, heeding the life and light of Christ. This comes right to the heart of our faith. The life that pleases God is not a set of religious duties; it is to hear His voice and obey His word. Meditation opens the door to this way of living."

The Christian practice of meditation is, at its core, ruminating on the word of God. Meditation creates space for the Spirit to speak directly to our hearts and apply God's word to our lives. When we ruminate on a passage of Scripture like Lamentations 3:22, *"The steadfast love of the Lord never ceases; his mercies never come to an end,"* we give God space to reveal all the ways in which his mercy and steadfast love are available to us. Meditation creates a pathway for Scripture to go past our minds and affect change within our hearts.

Another powerful aspect of Christian meditation is mulling over the character of God. Sometimes when I feel hopeless I will take a few passages of Scripture

about the hope God provides and meditate on them. And in the process of meditating on God's perfect character my thoughts, perspectives, and emotions come in line with the unchanging nature of my heavenly Father. Meditating on who God is powerfully affects the way we view the world. It's for this reason Psalm 1:1-3 declares,

Blessed is the man who walks not in the counsel of the wicked, nor stands in the way of sinners, nor sits in the seat of scoffers; but his delight is in the law of the Lord, and on his law he meditates day and night. He is like a tree planted by streams of water that yields its fruit in its season, and its leaf does not wither. In all that he does, he prospers.

Take time to meditate on Scripture today. Make space to listen to God and apply the seed of his word. Ruminate on his unchanging, perfect character. May your day be filled with abundant life as you bear the fruit of meditation.

131

GUIDED PRAYER

1. Choose a verse or aspect of God's character to meditate on.

2. Make space to hear from God as you meditate on his word or character. Allow the Spirit to apply God's word to your life as you meditate. Allow God's character to lay a foundation for your emotions.

"I will meditate on your precepts and fix my eyes on your ways." Psalm 119:15

3. Now take note of how the verse or phrase seems to have made an impact in the way you think, feel, or desire to act. Rejoice in the power of God's word to transform lives and hearts.

Meditation should be a daily practice for Christians. God's word was never meant to just be understood but to be alive and active in his children. Scripture is meant to direct us into becoming more like Jesus both internally and externally in our actions. Meditating is one of the best tools God has given us in taking the Bible from words on a page to a living and active lifestyle. May engaging in meditation transform your spiritual life into one filled with joy, power and fruit of the Spirit.

Extended Reading: Psalm 1

God Speaks in Solitude

DEVOTIONAL

Solitude—a time set apart where the rush, noise, and anxiety of the world fall mute on the ears and heart of a child of God completely lost in the peace and presence of the Creator. Solitude is a time to be with your heavenly Father, free from the distractions the world offers us at seemingly every moment. We are made for consistent time spent in solitude.

C.S. Lewis wrote in *The Weight of Glory*, "We live, in fact, in a world starved for solitude, silence, and private: and therefore starved for meditation and true friendship." Most of us have

"Be still, and know that I am God."

PSALM 46:10

grown accustomed to what truly does amount to being "starved" for solitude. We never fully realize how great our need is to be alone with our Sustainer. Let's take some time today to recognize our need for solitude and then learn how to best practice solitude on a daily basis.

You can know that you need solitude for one reason— Jesus needed it. All over the New Testament we see examples of Jesus going off on his own to pray. One example, Mark 1:35, tells us that Jesus, *"rising very early in the morning, while it was still dark . . . departed and went out to a desolate place, and there he prayed."* Jesus, who practiced perfect communion with his heavenly Father while here on earth still needed to spend time in solitude. Jesus, who loved parties, loved people, and was God and man simultaneously, needed time alone. If he needed it, you and I can be sure we need it. When God incarnate was up against his hardest task, the Crucifixion, he didn't just toughen up and get through it. He spent time alone in the Garden of Gethsemane in conversation with his heavenly Father. He needed solitude to accomplish his purpose here on earth and so do you and I.

Solitude is life-giving. It's necessary to the Christian spiritual life. Richard J. Foster said, "Loneliness is inner emptiness. Solitude is inner fulfillment." Solitude is one of the most important and life-giving spiritual disciplines. If you want to hear God, you must practice

solitude. If you want fortitude in your life, a steadfastness that surpasses your circumstances, you must practice solitude. You are designed for time spent in the quiet, simply being with your heavenly Father.

So how can you best practice solitude? The first step is finding a place where you can spend time with God free from distractions. Find a place where you know you won't be interrupted. If you live with others, find a time when they will not be around or awake. If you live alone, designate a place and time that you will spend in solitude free from any distractions. Second, give yourself an amount of time to spend with God just being in solitude. It could be ten minutes or an hour. Spend this time free from reading, free from worship or prayer unless solitude leads you to those things. Madeleine L'Engle said, "Deepest communion with God is beyond words, on the other side of silence." Solitude is a point of deep communion where words aren't required in light of God's glorious nearness.

Take some time today to practice the incredible discipline of solitude. Be patient with yourself. Be patient with God. Fill the emptiness of silence with the satisfaction of God's presence. Your heavenly Father loves just simply spending time with you, enjoying deep communion with his crown of creation. You are his child. Climb into the comforting and sustaining arms of your heavenly Father today as you enter into a time of solitude.

GUIDED PRAYER

1. Find a place free from distractions. Ask the Spirit to calm your heart and mind and help you to spend time in deep communion with God.

2. Spend a few minutes simply resting with God in solitude.

"And rising very early in the morning, while it was still dark, he departed and went out to a desolate place, and there he prayed." Mark 1:35

"Deepest communion with God is beyond words, on the other side of silence." Madeleine L'Engle

3. Write down how solitude made you feel. If you felt uncomfortable or frustrated, that's alright! Solitude and silence is something most of us have never practiced. Have patience with yourself.

Solitude is a practice. The more you do it the better and more fulfilling it will become. Once you connect with God's heart free of words and just look at him face to face, his gaze will become one of the most important parts of your life. Knowing experientially that your heavenly Father sees you and loves you is meant to be at the foundation of everything you do. Commit yourself to spend time in solitude with God and learn what it is to be a child simply enjoyed by the Father.

Extended Reading: Psalm 46

Receiving God's Word through Action

DAY 28

SCRIPTURE

"For if anyone is a hearer of the word and not a doer, he is like a man who looks intently at his natural face in a mirror. For he looks at himself and goes away and at once forgets what he was like. But the one who looks into the perfect law, the law of liberty, and perseveres, being no hearer who forgets but a doer who acts, he will be blessed in his doing." James 1:23-25

DEVOTIONAL

Faith and action go together. Understanding and works are tethered—joined together at salvation through the working of the Holy Spirit in the lives of believers. James 2:14-17 asks us,

What good is it, my brothers, if someone says he has faith but does not have works? Can that faith save him? If a brother or sister is poorly clothed and lacking in daily food, and one of you says to them, "Go in peace, be warmed and filled," without giving them the things needed for the body, what good is that? So also faith by itself, if it does not have works, is dead.

The poor, orphaned, widowed, and lost don't just need a word from God. They need us to act on our beliefs and love and serve selflessly with the help of the Holy Spirit. Gathering together as believers to worship is just a part of what God intends for us as his children. If we are to receive all that God has for us, if we are to walk in the abundant life God intends, we must resolve to be doers of the word.

James 1:23-25 gives us a window into the life of a believer who never puts action to his faith. Scripture says,

For if anyone is a hearer of the word and not a doer, he is like a man who looks intently at his natural face in a

mirror. For he looks at himself and goes away and at once forgets what he was like. But the one who looks into the perfect law, the law of liberty, and perseveres, being no hearer who forgets but a doer who acts, he will be blessed in his doing.

Your identity as a disciple of Christ undoubtedly comes from relationship with God, but it is meant to be lived out in your deeds. God longs for you to live a life of good works in response to the unconditional love you've been given. He longs for you to live in selfless humility sharing with others what he's done in you.

We've separated Christianity from the world. We've separated Sunday from Monday, the sacred and secular. Jesus lived in line with God's love every minute he was here. He broke the rules in healing on the Sabbath. He ministered almost completely outside of the walls of the synagogue. He brought the good news of God's grace to all who would believe everywhere he went. His life was in no way segregated. Jesus's turning the water into wine at a party was just as holy and spiritual as his reading of Isaiah in the temple, proclaiming his fulfillment of the prophecy regarding the Messiah. His love was put into perfect action through every word, miracle, step, glance, and prayer.

With Jesus as our perfect example, let's live in accordance with God's will. Let's blur the line of faith and works until the two become one. Let's regard meals, conversations, rest, family time, and parties as important and holy as worshipping inside the walls of our churches. Let's live as Jesus did and make love an action instead of just an idea we talk about on Sunday.

GUIDED PRAYER

1. Meditate on God's desire for your faith to produce good works.

"What good is it, my brothers, if someone says he has faith but does not have works? Can that faith save him? If a brother or sister is poorly clothed and lacking in daily food, and one of you says to them, 'Go in peace, be warmed and filled,' without giving them the things needed for the body, what good is that? So also faith by itself, if it does not have works, is dead." James 2:14-17

2. Ask God where he would have you put faith into action. It could be buying flowers for your wife, finding a new way to honor your husband, taking your children on a special trip, or offering encouragement to someone around you at work or school. Ask the Spirit to give you specific ways in which he desires you live out the love you have received.

3. Ask God for the strength and courage to live out his word. Follow the leadership of the Spirit into the good works he has prepared for you today.

The Spirit has an incredible ability and power to guide a willing heart into action for God. Receiving the knowledge of God's love for the people around you will open up doors in your own life to better know the fullness of God's heart. You will be more deeply blessed by serving others than you could ever be blessed in being served. God pours his love and grace out on those who minister in line with the leading of the Spirit. It's truly an honor to be used by God to further the advance of his kingdom in the earth. You were made to live out the truth of the gospel. So choose today to act upon the leading of the Spirit. Choose to be a doer of the word.

Extended Reading: James 1